Beyond the Broken Mind: A Journey to Triumph Over Schizophrenia

Travis Breeding

Published by Travis Breeding, 2024.

BEYOND THE BROKEN MIND: A JOURNEY TO TRIUMPH OVER SCHIZOPHRENIA

First edition. February 22, 2024.

ISBN: 979-8224111442

Written by Travis Breeding.

Also by Travis Breeding

Watch for more at breedingautismconsulting.com.

Table of Contents

Chapter 1: Inside the Mind of Schizophrenia: A Comprehensive Guide

Schizophrenia is a chronic and severe mental disorder that affects how a person thinks, feels, and behaves. It is a complex condition that can have a profound impact on individuals and society as a whole. People with schizophrenia often experience symptoms such as hallucinations, delusions, disorganized speech, and cognitive difficulties. These symptoms can make it challenging for individuals to function in their daily lives and maintain relationships.

The impact of schizophrenia extends beyond the individual affected by the disorder. It can also have significant effects on families, caregivers, and society as a whole. The economic burden of schizophrenia is substantial, with costs associated with treatment, hospitalization, and lost productivity. Additionally, stigma and discrimination surrounding mental illness can further isolate individuals with schizophrenia and prevent them from seeking the help they need.

Understanding Schizophrenia: An Overview

Schizophrenia is a chronic mental disorder characterized by a range of symptoms that affect a person's thoughts, emotions, and behavior. It typically begins in late adolescence or early adulthood and can persist throughout a person's life. The exact cause of schizophrenia is unknown, but it is believed to be a combination of genetic, environmental, and neurobiological factors.

There are several different types of schizophrenia, including paranoid schizophrenia, disorganized schizophrenia, catatonic schizophrenia, residual schizophrenia, and undifferentiated schizophrenia. Each type has its own unique set of symptoms and characteristics.

The prevalence of schizophrenia varies across different populations and countries. According to the World Health Organization (WHO), approximately 20 million people worldwide have schizophrenia. The incidence rate is estimated to be around 15 cases per 100,000 people per year.

Historically, schizophrenia has been surrounded by stigma and misunderstanding. People with schizophrenia have often been portrayed as dangerous or unpredictable in the media and popular culture. This stigma can lead to discrimination and social exclusion, making it even more difficult for individuals with schizophrenia to seek help and receive appropriate treatment.

Symptoms of Schizophrenia: What to Look Out for

Schizophrenia is characterized by a range of symptoms that can be categorized into three main groups: positive symptoms, negative symptoms, and cognitive symptoms.

Positive symptoms are those that are not typically present in healthy individuals but are present in people with schizophrenia. These symptoms include hallucinations, which are sensory experiences that are not based in reality, such as hearing voices or seeing things that are not there. Delusions, which are false beliefs that are firmly held despite evidence to the contrary, are also common in schizophrenia. Disorganized speech, such as speaking incoherently or jumping from one topic to another, is another positive symptom.

Negative symptoms refer to a lack of normal behaviors or emotions. These can include a lack of motivation or interest in activities, social withdrawal and isolation, and a flat affect, which is a reduced range of emotional expression. Negative symptoms can be particularly debilitating and can make it difficult for individuals with schizophrenia to engage in daily activities and maintain relationships.

Cognitive symptoms of schizophrenia can include problems with memory, attention, and executive functioning. Individuals with schizophrenia may have difficulty concentrating, organizing their thoughts, and making decisions. These cognitive impairments can significantly impact a person's ability to work or go to school.

The Causes of Schizophrenia: Genetics, Environment, and More

The exact cause of schizophrenia is still unknown, but research suggests that it is likely a combination of genetic, environmental, and neurobiological factors.

Genetic factors play a significant role in the development of schizophrenia. Studies have shown that individuals who have a first-degree relative with schizophrenia have a higher risk of developing the disorder themselves. The heritability of schizophrenia is estimated to be around 80%, indicating that genetic factors contribute significantly to its development.

Environmental factors also play a role in the development of schizophrenia. Prenatal exposure to certain infections, complications during pregnancy or birth, and exposure to stress or trauma during childhood have all been associated with an increased risk of developing schizophrenia. Additionally, growing up in an urban environment has been linked to a higher risk of developing the disorder.

Neurobiological factors, such as abnormalities in brain structure and neurotransmitter imbalances, are also believed to contribute to the development of schizophrenia. The dopamine hypothesis suggests that an overactivity of dopamine in certain areas of the brain may be responsible for the positive symptoms of schizophrenia. Structural abnormalities in the brain, such as enlarged ventricles or reduced gray matter volume, have also been observed in individuals with schizophrenia.

Diagnosing Schizophrenia: What to Expect

Diagnosing schizophrenia can be challenging because there is no definitive test or biomarker for the disorder. Instead, diagnosis is based on a thorough evaluation of a person's symptoms and history.

The Diagnostic and Statistical Manual of Mental Disorders (DSM-5) provides criteria for diagnosing schizophrenia. To meet the criteria for a diagnosis, a person must experience at least two of the following symptoms for a significant portion of time during a one-month period: delusions, hallucinations, disorganized speech, grossly disorganized or catatonic behavior, or negative symptoms. Additionally, the person must experience a decline in functioning and have symptoms that persist for at least six months.

In addition to a clinical interview, other assessments may be used to aid in the diagnosis of schizophrenia. These can include psychological tests, neuroimaging studies, and laboratory tests to rule out other medical conditions that may be causing the symptoms.

Early detection and intervention are crucial for individuals with schizophrenia. Research has shown that early treatment can lead to better outcomes and improved quality of life. If you suspect that you or someone you know may have schizophrenia, it is important to seek help from a mental health professional as soon as possible.

Living with Schizophrenia: Coping Strategies and Support

Living with schizophrenia can be challenging, but there are strategies and support systems that can help individuals manage their symptoms and improve their quality of life.

Self-care strategies are an essential part of managing schizophrenia. Regular exercise has been shown to have a positive impact on mental health and can help reduce symptoms of schizophrenia. A healthy diet, rich in fruits, vegetables, whole grains, and lean proteins, can also support overall well-being. Stress management techniques, such as mindfulness meditation or deep breathing exercises, can help individuals cope with the challenges of living with schizophrenia.

Social support is also crucial for individuals with schizophrenia. Family and friends can provide emotional support and practical assistance in managing symptoms and daily activities. Support groups, either in-person or online, can connect individuals with others who are going through similar experiences and provide a sense of community.

Vocational and educational support is also important for individuals with schizophrenia. Many people with schizophrenia are able to work or attend school with the right accommodations and support. Vocational rehabilitation programs can provide job training and assistance in finding employment. Educational support services can help students with schizophrenia succeed in school by providing accommodations and resources.

Medications for Schizophrenia: How They Work and Side Effects

Medications are a cornerstone of treatment for schizophrenia. Antipsychotic medications are the most commonly prescribed medications for schizophrenia and work by reducing the symptoms of psychosis.

There are two main types of antipsychotic medications: typical antipsychotics and atypical antipsychotics. Typical antipsychotics, such as haloperidol or chlorpromazine, work by blocking dopamine receptors in the brain. Atypical antipsychotics, such as risperidone or olanzapine, also block dopamine receptors but also affect other neurotransmitters, such as serotonin.

The exact mechanisms of action of antipsychotic medications are not fully understood, but they are believed to work by reducing the activity of dopamine in certain areas of the brain. This helps to alleviate the positive symptoms of schizophrenia, such as hallucinations and delusions.

While antipsychotic medications can be effective in reducing symptoms, they can also have side effects. Common side effects of antipsychotics include weight gain, sedation, and movement disorders such as tremors or stiffness. It is important for individuals taking antipsychotic medications to work closely with their healthcare provider to monitor for side effects and adjust the medication as needed.

Therapy for Schizophrenia: Types and Benefits

In addition to medication, therapy is an important component of treatment for schizophrenia. Therapy can help individuals with schizophrenia learn coping strategies, improve their social skills, and manage their symptoms.

Cognitive-behavioral therapy (CBT) is a type of therapy that focuses on identifying and changing negative thought patterns and behaviors. CBT can help individuals with schizophrenia challenge their delusions or hallucinations and develop more adaptive ways of thinking and behaving.

Family therapy can also be beneficial for individuals with schizophrenia. Family therapy involves working with the individual's family members to improve communication, reduce stress, and provide support. Family members can learn about the symptoms of schizophrenia and how to best support their loved one.

Social skills training is another type of therapy that can be helpful for individuals with schizophrenia. This type of therapy focuses on teaching individuals how to interact with others, manage social situations, and improve their communication skills. Social skills training can help individuals with schizophrenia build confidence and improve their relationships.

Therapy can have many benefits for individuals with schizophrenia. It can help reduce symptoms, improve functioning, and enhance overall quality of life. It is important for individuals with schizophrenia to work closely with a mental health professional to determine which type of therapy is most appropriate for their needs.

Schizophrenia and Substance Abuse: A Dangerous Combination

There is a high rate of comorbidity between schizophrenia and substance abuse. Research has shown that individuals with schizophrenia are more likely to use drugs or alcohol compared to the general population.

The reasons for the high rates of substance abuse among individuals with schizophrenia are complex. Some individuals may use substances as a way to self-medicate or alleviate their symptoms. Others may be more vulnerable to substance abuse due to genetic or environmental factors.

The combination of schizophrenia and substance abuse can have serious consequences. Substance abuse can worsen the symptoms of schizophrenia and increase the risk of relapse and hospitalization. It can also interfere with the effectiveness of medications and make it more difficult for individuals to engage in treatment.

Integrated treatment that addresses both the symptoms of schizophrenia and substance abuse is crucial for individuals with co-occurring disorders. This may involve a combination of medication, therapy, and support groups that specifically address substance abuse. It is important for individuals with schizophrenia and substance abuse issues to seek help from a mental health professional who specializes in dual diagnosis treatment.

Schizophrenia and Violence: Separating Fact from Fiction

There are many myths and misconceptions surrounding schizophrenia and violence. Contrary to popular belief, individuals with schizophrenia are not inherently violent or dangerous. In fact, research has shown that individuals with schizophrenia are more likely to be victims of violence rather than perpetrators.

The media often portrays individuals with schizophrenia as violent or unpredictable, perpetuating these stereotypes. This stigma can have serious consequences, leading to discrimination, social isolation, and barriers to treatment.

The actual rates of violence among individuals with schizophrenia are relatively low. Studies have shown that the vast majority of individuals with schizophrenia are not violent and pose no threat to others. However, certain factors, such as substance abuse or a history of violence, can increase the risk of violent behavior in individuals with schizophrenia.

It is important to address stigma and discrimination surrounding mental illness, including schizophrenia. Education and awareness can help dispel myths and promote understanding and empathy. By challenging stereotypes and promoting a more accurate understanding of schizophrenia, we can create a more inclusive and supportive society for individuals with mental illness.

Schizophrenia and Suicide: Risks and Prevention

Individuals with schizophrenia are at a higher risk of suicide compared to the general population. Studies have shown that the lifetime risk of suicide among individuals with schizophrenia is approximately 5-10%.

There are several risk factors that contribute to the increased risk of suicide among individuals with schizophrenia. These can include a history of suicide attempts, a family history of suicide, comorbid depression or substance abuse, and social isolation.

It is important to be aware of the warning signs of suicide in individuals with schizophrenia. These can include talking about death or suicide, expressing feelings of hopelessness or worthlessness, withdrawing from social activities, and giving away possessions.

Prevention strategies for suicide in individuals with schizophrenia include early detection and intervention, access to mental health services, and support from family and friends. It is important for individuals with schizophrenia to have a safety plan in place that includes emergency contact information and strategies for managing suicidal thoughts.

If you or someone you know is experiencing suicidal thoughts, it is important to seek help immediately. Contact a mental health professional or call a helpline in your country for assistance.

The Future of Schizophrenia Treatment: Promising Research and Developments

Research into the causes and treatment of schizophrenia is ongoing, and there are several promising developments on the horizon.

Advances in pharmacological treatments are being made, with researchers exploring new medications that target specific neurotransmitter systems in the brain. These medications may have fewer side effects and be more effective in reducing symptoms.

Emerging therapies, such as neurostimulation and virtual reality, are also being explored as potential treatments for schizophrenia. Neurostimulation techniques, such as transcranial magnetic stimulation (TMS) or deep brain stimulation (DBS), involve using electrical or magnetic pulses to stimulate specific areas of the brain. Virtual reality therapy uses immersive technology to create simulated environments that can help individuals with schizophrenia practice social skills and manage their symptoms.

Continued research and advocacy are crucial for improving the lives of individuals with schizophrenia. By supporting research efforts and advocating for increased funding and resources, we can help advance our understanding of schizophrenia and develop more effective treatments.

Schizophrenia is a complex and challenging mental disorder that affects millions of people worldwide. It can have a profound impact on individuals, families, and society as a whole. Understanding the symptoms, causes, and treatment options for schizophrenia is crucial for providing support and improving outcomes for individuals with the disorder.

By promoting awareness, challenging stigma, and advocating for increased resources and support, we can create a more inclusive and supportive society for individuals with schizophrenia. With continued research and advancements in treatment, there is hope for improved outcomes and a brighter future for individuals living with schizophrenia.

Chapter 2: 10 Effective Coping Strategies for Dealing with Stress and Anxiety

In today's fast-paced and demanding world, stress and anxiety have become increasingly prevalent. Whether it's due to work pressures, financial concerns, or personal relationships, many individuals find themselves struggling to cope with the overwhelming feelings that stress and anxiety can bring. The negative impact of these mental health issues on both our mental and physical well-being cannot be overstated. That is why it is crucial to develop effective coping strategies to manage stress and anxiety.

Stress and anxiety can take a toll on our mental health, leading to symptoms such as irritability, difficulty concentrating, and even depression. Additionally, chronic stress has been linked to physical health problems such as high blood pressure, heart disease, and weakened immune function. It is clear that finding ways to effectively manage stress and anxiety is essential for maintaining overall health and well-being.

Coping strategies are techniques or activities that individuals can use to help them deal with stress and anxiety. These strategies can vary from person to person, as what works for one individual may not work for another. However, the importance of finding effective coping strategies cannot be overstated. By developing healthy ways to manage stress and anxiety, individuals can improve their mental and physical health, enhance their overall quality of life, and build resilience in the face of future challenges.

Mindfulness Meditation: A Powerful Tool for Managing Stress and Anxiety

One coping strategy that has gained significant attention in recent years is mindfulness meditation. Mindfulness meditation involves focusing one's attention on the present moment without judgment. It encourages individuals to observe their thoughts and feelings without getting caught up in them.

The benefits of mindfulness meditation for stress and anxiety are well-documented. Research has shown that regular practice of mindfulness meditation can reduce symptoms of anxiety and depression, improve attention and focus, enhance self-awareness, and promote overall well-being. By cultivating a non-judgmental and accepting attitude towards one's thoughts and emotions, individuals can learn to respond to stress and anxiety in a more calm and balanced manner.

To practice mindfulness meditation, find a quiet and comfortable space where you can sit or lie down. Close your eyes and take a few deep breaths to relax your body. Begin by focusing your attention on your breath, noticing the sensation of the breath as it enters and leaves your body. If your mind wanders, gently bring your attention back to the breath without judgment. You can start with just a few minutes of practice each day and gradually increase the duration as you become more comfortable.

Exercise and Physical Activity: The Benefits of Staying Active to Reduce Stress

Exercise and physical activity have long been recognized as effective coping strategies for managing stress and anxiety. Engaging in regular exercise not only improves physical fitness but also has a positive impact on mental health.

Numerous studies have shown that exercise can reduce symptoms of anxiety and depression, improve mood, boost self-esteem, and enhance overall well-being. Physical activity releases endorphins, which are natural mood-boosting chemicals in the brain. It also helps to reduce levels of stress hormones such as cortisol, leading to a decrease in feelings of stress and anxiety.

Different types of exercise can have varying benefits for stress and anxiety. Aerobic exercises such as running, swimming, or cycling are particularly effective in reducing anxiety symptoms. These activities increase heart rate and circulation, promoting the release of endorphins and providing a natural mood lift. Strength training exercises, on the other hand, can help individuals feel more empowered and confident, reducing feelings of stress and anxiety.

To incorporate exercise into your routine, find activities that you enjoy and that fit into your schedule. Aim for at least 150 minutes of moderate-intensity aerobic activity or 75 minutes of vigorous-intensity aerobic activity per week, along with strength training exercises at least twice a week. Remember that even small amounts of physical activity can have a positive impact on stress and anxiety, so start with what feels manageable and gradually increase your activity level.

Deep Breathing Techniques: How to Use Breathing Exercises to Calm Your Mind

Deep breathing techniques are simple yet powerful tools for managing stress and anxiety. When we are stressed or anxious, our breathing tends to become shallow and rapid. This can further exacerbate feelings of stress and anxiety. Deep breathing exercises help to activate the body's relaxation response, promoting a sense of calm and reducing the physiological symptoms of stress.

The science behind deep breathing and stress reduction lies in its impact on the autonomic nervous system. Deep breathing activates the parasympathetic nervous system, which is responsible for the body's rest and digest response. This helps to counteract the effects of the sympathetic nervous system, which is responsible for the body's fight or flight response.

There are various types of breathing exercises that can be used to manage stress and anxiety. One simple technique is diaphragmatic breathing, also known as belly breathing. To practice this technique, sit or lie down in a comfortable position. Place one hand on your chest and the other on your abdomen. Take a slow, deep breath in through your nose, allowing your abdomen to rise as you fill your lungs with air. Exhale slowly through your mouth, allowing your abdomen to fall as you release the breath. Repeat this process several times, focusing on the sensation of your breath as it enters and leaves your body.

Cognitive Behavioral Therapy: A Proven Approach to Managing Stress and Anxiety

Cognitive Behavioral Therapy (CBT) is a widely recognized and evidence-based approach to managing stress and anxiety. CBT focuses on identifying and changing negative thought patterns and behaviors that contribute to stress and anxiety.

The goal of CBT is to help individuals develop healthier ways of thinking and responding to stressors. By challenging negative thoughts and replacing them with more realistic and positive ones, individuals can reduce their levels of stress and anxiety. CBT also involves learning and practicing coping skills to manage stress more effectively.

To find a cognitive behavioral therapist, start by asking your primary care physician for a referral. You can also search online directories or contact your insurance provider for a list of covered providers. It is important to find a therapist who is experienced in treating stress and anxiety and with whom you feel comfortable. Remember that therapy is a collaborative process, so be open and honest with your therapist about your goals and concerns.

Social Support: The Importance of Having a Strong Support System

Social support plays a crucial role in managing stress and anxiety. Having a strong support system can provide individuals with emotional validation, practical assistance, and a sense of belonging. It can also help to reduce feelings of isolation and loneliness, which are common in individuals experiencing stress and anxiety.

Building and maintaining a strong support system involves nurturing relationships with family, friends, and other supportive individuals in your life. This can be done through regular communication, spending quality time together, and being open and honest about your feelings and needs. It is important to surround yourself with people who are understanding, empathetic, and non-judgmental.

Support groups can also be a valuable resource for individuals managing stress and anxiety. These groups provide a safe space for individuals to share their experiences, learn from others, and gain support from individuals who are going through similar challenges. Support groups can be found through community organizations, mental health clinics, or online platforms.

Time Management: Strategies for Prioritizing Tasks and Reducing Stress

Time management is another important coping strategy for managing stress and anxiety. When we feel overwhelmed by the demands of our daily lives, it can contribute to feelings of stress and anxiety. By effectively managing our time, we can prioritize tasks, reduce procrastination, and create a sense of control and balance.

The link between time management and stress reduction lies in the ability to prioritize tasks and allocate time for self-care activities. By identifying the most important and urgent tasks, individuals can focus their energy and attention on completing them. This can help to reduce feelings of overwhelm and increase productivity.

To manage your time effectively, start by creating a schedule or to-do list. Prioritize tasks based on their importance and deadline. Break larger tasks into smaller, more manageable steps. Set realistic goals and deadlines for yourself, allowing for breaks and self-care activities. Remember to be flexible and adaptable, as unexpected events or changes in priorities may arise.

Journaling: How Writing Can Help You Process Your Thoughts and Feelings

Journaling is a powerful tool for managing stress and anxiety. Writing down our thoughts and feelings can help us gain clarity, process emotions, and gain a new perspective on our challenges. Journaling provides a safe space for self-reflection and self-expression.

The benefits of journaling for stress and anxiety are numerous. It can help individuals identify triggers for stress and anxiety, explore patterns of thinking and behavior, and develop strategies for coping with challenges. Journaling can also serve as a form of self-care, providing individuals with an outlet for their emotions and a way to practice gratitude and positivity.

There are different types of journaling techniques that individuals can try. Free writing involves writing continuously without censoring or editing your thoughts. This allows for a free flow of ideas and emotions onto the page. Reflective journaling involves writing about specific experiences or events, exploring their impact on your thoughts, feelings, and behaviors. Gratitude journaling involves writing down things that you are grateful for each day, focusing on the positive aspects of your life.

To get started with journaling, find a quiet space where you can write without distractions. Set aside a specific time each day or week for journaling. Write freely and honestly, without worrying about grammar or spelling. Remember that journaling is a personal practice, so there is no right or wrong way to do it. Experiment with different techniques and find what works best for you.

Relaxation Techniques: The Power of Activities Like Yoga and Massage

Relaxation techniques such as yoga and massage can be effective coping strategies for managing stress and anxiety. These activities promote relaxation, reduce muscle tension, and calm the mind.

The benefits of relaxation techniques for stress and anxiety are well-documented. Yoga, for example, combines physical postures, breathing exercises, and meditation to promote relaxation and reduce stress. It has been shown to improve mood, reduce anxiety symptoms, and enhance overall well-being. Massage therapy involves the manipulation of soft tissues in the body to promote relaxation and relieve muscle tension. It can help individuals feel more grounded, reduce physical symptoms of stress, and improve sleep quality.

To incorporate relaxation techniques into your routine, start by exploring different activities that you enjoy. Consider joining a yoga class or finding online resources to guide your practice. Schedule regular massage appointments or learn self-massage techniques that you can do at home. Remember that relaxation is a personal experience, so find activities that resonate with you and make you feel calm and centered.

Mindset Shifts: Changing Your Perspective to Better Manage Stress and Anxiety

Our mindset plays a crucial role in how we perceive and respond to stress and anxiety. By cultivating a positive mindset and adopting certain mindset shifts, individuals can better manage their stress and anxiety.

One mindset shift involves reframing negative thoughts into more positive ones. For example, instead of thinking "I can't handle this," try reframing it as "I am capable of handling this challenge." This shift in perspective can help individuals feel more empowered and confident in their ability to cope with stressors.

Another mindset shift involves practicing self-compassion. Instead of being self-critical or judgmental, individuals can learn to be kind and understanding towards themselves. This involves acknowledging and accepting their feelings and experiences without judgment. Self-compassion can help individuals feel more supported and less alone in their struggles with stress and anxiety.

To cultivate a positive mindset, practice gratitude and mindfulness. Take time each day to reflect on the things you are grateful for, no matter how small. This can help shift your focus from negative thoughts to positive ones. Practice mindfulness by bringing your attention to the present moment without judgment. This can help you become more aware of your thoughts and emotions, allowing you to respond to stress and anxiety in a more calm and balanced manner.

Putting These Coping Strategies into Practice in Your Everyday Life

In conclusion, managing stress and anxiety is essential for maintaining overall health and well-being. By developing effective coping strategies, individuals can reduce the negative impact of stress and anxiety on their mental and physical health.

It is important to find coping strategies that work for you as an individual. Experiment with different techniques and activities to see what resonates with you. Remember that what works for one person may not work for another, so be open to trying new things.

Incorporating coping strategies into your daily routine is key to their effectiveness. Set aside time each day or week to practice mindfulness meditation, engage in physical activity, or journal your thoughts and feelings. Prioritize self-care activities and make them a non-negotiable part of your schedule.

The benefits of managing stress and anxiety are numerous. By developing healthy coping strategies, individuals can improve their mental and physical health, enhance their overall quality of life, and build resilience in the face of future challenges. Take the first step towards managing stress and anxiety today by incorporating these coping strategies into your everyday life.

Chapter 3: The Benefits of Psychoeducation: Empowering Individuals to Take Control of Their Mental Health

Psychoeducation is a crucial component of mental health treatment that aims to provide individuals with the knowledge and skills they need to understand and manage their mental health conditions. It involves educating individuals about their specific mental health condition, its symptoms, treatment options, and strategies for self-care and self-management. By empowering individuals with information and resources, psychoeducation helps them take an active role in their own mental health care and improve their overall well-being.

Understanding the Concept of Psychoeducation

Psychoeducation can be defined as the process of providing education and information about mental health conditions to individuals, their families, and the community. It aims to increase awareness and understanding of mental health issues, reduce stigma, and promote early intervention and effective treatment. The goals of psychoeducation include improving knowledge about mental health conditions, enhancing coping skills, promoting self-advocacy, reducing symptoms, preventing relapse, and improving overall functioning.

There are different approaches to psychoeducation, depending on the specific needs of individuals and the context in which it is being delivered. It can be provided in individual or group settings, through workshops, support groups, or online platforms. The content of psychoeducation programs may vary but typically includes information about the nature of mental health conditions, available treatment options, strategies for managing symptoms, and resources for support.

The Importance of Psychoeducation in Mental Health Treatment

Psychoeducation plays a crucial role in mental health treatment for several reasons. Firstly, it provides individuals with a better understanding of their mental health condition, its symptoms, and how it affects their daily lives. This knowledge helps individuals make informed decisions about their treatment options and empowers them to take an active role in managing their symptoms.

Secondly, psychoeducation has been shown to reduce symptoms and improve overall functioning in individuals with mental illness. By providing individuals with strategies for managing their symptoms and promoting self-care, psychoeducation helps individuals develop the skills they need to cope with their condition and improve their quality of life.

Lastly, psychoeducation is important in preventing relapse. By educating individuals about the early warning signs of relapse and providing them with strategies for preventing and managing relapse, psychoeducation helps individuals stay on track with their treatment and maintain their mental health.

Empowering Individuals to Take Control of Their Mental Health

One of the key benefits of psychoeducation is that it empowers individuals to take control of their mental health. By providing individuals with information about their condition and strategies for managing their symptoms, psychoeducation helps individuals develop a sense of self-efficacy and self-advocacy.

Self-care and self-management are crucial aspects of mental health treatment. Psychoeducation equips individuals with the knowledge and skills they need to engage in self-care activities such as maintaining a healthy lifestyle, practicing stress management techniques, and seeking support when needed. By promoting self-care and self-management, psychoeducation helps individuals take an active role in their own mental health care and improve their overall well-being.

Strategies for promoting self-efficacy and self-advocacy include setting realistic goals, developing problem-solving skills, practicing assertiveness, and seeking support from others. By encouraging individuals to take ownership of their mental health, psychoeducation helps them build resilience and develop a sense of empowerment.

Reducing Stigma and Promoting Mental Health Awareness

Stigma surrounding mental illness is a significant barrier to seeking help and receiving appropriate treatment. Psychoeducation plays a crucial role in reducing stigma and promoting mental health awareness by providing accurate information about mental health conditions and challenging misconceptions.

One strategy for addressing stigma is through education and outreach programs that aim to increase awareness and understanding of mental health issues. These programs can be targeted towards schools, workplaces, community organizations, and healthcare providers. By providing accurate information about mental health conditions, these programs help dispel myths and misconceptions and promote a more compassionate and supportive attitude towards individuals with mental illness.

Another strategy for reducing stigma is through storytelling and personal narratives. By sharing their experiences, individuals with mental illness can challenge stereotypes and humanize the condition, helping to reduce fear and discrimination. Psychoeducation programs can provide a platform for individuals to share their stories and raise awareness about mental health issues.

Enhancing Coping Skills and Resilience

Psychoeducation can enhance coping skills and resilience in individuals with mental illness. Coping skills are strategies that individuals use to manage stress, regulate emotions, and navigate challenging situations. By providing individuals with a range of coping strategies, psychoeducation helps them develop healthier ways of dealing with stressors and managing their symptoms.

Some common coping strategies that may be taught in psychoeducation programs include relaxation techniques, mindfulness exercises, problem-solving skills, and social support. These strategies help individuals build resilience and improve their ability to cope with the challenges of living with a mental health condition.

Promoting resilience and emotional well-being is an important aspect of psychoeducation. Resilience refers to an individual's ability to bounce back from adversity and maintain positive mental health. By providing individuals with the tools they need to build resilience, psychoeducation helps them develop a strong foundation for recovery and well-being.

Improving Treatment Adherence and Outcomes

Psychoeducation plays a crucial role in improving treatment adherence and outcomes for individuals with mental illness. Treatment adherence refers to the extent to which individuals follow their prescribed treatment plan, including taking medication as prescribed, attending therapy sessions, and engaging in self-care activities.

One of the key factors that contribute to treatment non-adherence is a lack of understanding about the nature of mental health conditions and the importance of treatment. Psychoeducation helps address this issue by providing individuals with information about their condition, its treatment options, and the potential benefits of adhering to treatment.

Importance of medication management and adherence is another aspect of psychoeducation. Many individuals with mental illness are prescribed medication as part of their treatment plan. However, medication non-adherence is a common problem, which can lead to worsening symptoms and increased risk of relapse. Psychoeducation programs can provide individuals with information about the importance of taking medication as prescribed, potential side effects, and strategies for managing medication effectively.

Strategies for promoting treatment adherence and positive outcomes include providing clear and concise information about treatment options, involving individuals in the decision-making process, addressing any concerns or misconceptions about treatment, and providing ongoing support and monitoring.

Promoting Self-Advocacy and Empowerment

Psychoeducation can promote self-advocacy and empowerment in individuals with mental illness. Self-advocacy refers to the ability to speak up for one's own needs and rights, make informed decisions about one's treatment, and actively participate in the treatment process.

Importance of advocating for one's own mental health needs is crucial in mental health treatment. By providing individuals with information about their condition, treatment options, and available resources, psychoeducation helps individuals become more informed consumers of mental health services. This knowledge empowers individuals to ask questions, seek second opinions, and make decisions that are in line with their own values and preferences.

Strategies for promoting self-advocacy and empowerment include providing individuals with information about their rights as patients, teaching effective communication skills, encouraging individuals to ask questions and seek clarification, and involving individuals in the development of their treatment plans.

Fostering Positive Relationships and Social Support

Psychoeducation plays a crucial role in fostering positive relationships and social support for individuals with mental illness. Social support refers to the emotional, instrumental, and informational assistance that individuals receive from others. It has been shown to be a protective factor against mental health problems and can enhance an individual's ability to cope with stress and manage their symptoms.

Importance of social support in mental health treatment cannot be overstated. By providing individuals with information about the benefits of social support and strategies for building and maintaining positive relationships, psychoeducation helps individuals develop a strong support network that can provide emotional support, practical assistance, and a sense of belonging.

Strategies for building and maintaining positive relationships include joining support groups, participating in community activities, reaching out to friends and family members, and seeking professional help when needed. Psychoeducation programs can provide individuals with the skills they need to develop and maintain healthy relationships, as well as strategies for seeking support when they need it.

Addressing Common Misconceptions and Myths About Mental Illness

There are many misconceptions and myths surrounding mental illness that can contribute to stigma and discrimination. Psychoeducation plays a crucial role in addressing these misconceptions and promoting accurate information about mental health conditions.

Some common misconceptions about mental illness include the belief that it is a sign of weakness or a character flaw, that individuals with mental illness are dangerous or unpredictable, or that they can simply "snap out of it" if they try hard enough. These misconceptions can lead to fear, discrimination, and a lack of understanding about the nature of mental health conditions.

Importance of addressing these misconceptions is crucial in promoting mental health literacy. By providing accurate information about mental health conditions, their causes, symptoms, and treatment options, psychoeducation helps dispel myths and challenge stereotypes. This can help reduce stigma and promote a more compassionate and supportive attitude towards individuals with mental illness.

Strategies for addressing misconceptions and promoting mental health literacy include providing accurate information through educational materials, workshops, and community outreach programs. It is also important to involve individuals with lived experience in these initiatives, as their personal stories can help challenge stereotypes and humanize the condition.

Enhancing Communication and Collaboration Between Patients and Providers

Effective communication between patients and healthcare providers is crucial in mental health treatment. Psychoeducation plays a crucial role in enhancing communication and collaboration between patients and providers by providing individuals with the skills they need to effectively communicate their needs, concerns, and preferences.

Importance of effective communication in mental health treatment cannot be overstated. By providing individuals with information about their condition, treatment options, and available resources, psychoeducation helps individuals become more informed consumers of mental health services. This knowledge empowers individuals to ask questions, seek second opinions, and make decisions that are in line with their own values and preferences.

Strategies for promoting effective communication and collaboration include teaching individuals effective communication skills, such as active listening, assertiveness, and expressing their needs and concerns. It is also important for healthcare providers to create a safe and supportive environment where individuals feel comfortable sharing their thoughts and feelings.

Integrating Psychoeducation into Comprehensive Mental Health Care

Integrating psychoeducation into comprehensive mental health care is crucial for ensuring that individuals receive the support and resources they need to manage their mental health effectively. Psychoeducation should be seen as an essential component of mental health treatment, alongside medication management, therapy, and other interventions.

Importance of integrating psychoeducation into comprehensive mental health care is that it provides individuals with the knowledge and skills they need to understand and manage their mental health conditions. By empowering individuals with information and resources, psychoeducation helps them take an active role in their own mental health care and improve their overall well-being.

Strategies for integrating psychoeducation into mental health treatment include incorporating psychoeducation into therapy sessions, providing educational materials and resources to individuals and their families, offering workshops or support groups focused on psychoeducation, and incorporating psychoeducation into community outreach programs.

Psychoeducation plays a crucial role in mental health treatment by providing individuals with the knowledge and skills they need to understand and manage their mental health conditions. It empowers individuals to take an active role in their own mental health care, reduces stigma, promotes mental health awareness, enhances coping skills and resilience, improves treatment adherence and outcomes, promotes self-advocacy and empowerment, fosters positive relationships and social support, addresses common misconceptions and myths about mental illness, enhances communication and collaboration between patients and providers, and integrates into comprehensive mental health care.

In order to promote psychoeducation and mental health literacy, it is important for healthcare providers, educators, policymakers, and community organizations to work together to develop and implement effective psychoeducation programs. By providing individuals with the knowledge and skills they need to understand and manage their mental health conditions, psychoeducation can help improve the lives of individuals with mental illness and promote a more compassionate and supportive society.

Chapter 4: Mastering Medication Management: Tips and Tricks for Staying on Track

Medication management plays a crucial role in maintaining good health. Whether you are taking prescription medications for a chronic condition or over-the-counter medications for occasional ailments, it is important to understand how to properly use and manage your medications. Improper medication use can lead to serious health risks and complications. By taking control of your medication management, you can ensure that you are using your medications safely and effectively.

Understanding Your Medications: Dosages, Side Effects, and Interactions

One of the key aspects of medication management is understanding your medications. This includes knowing the correct dosage of each medication you are taking. Taking too little or too much of a medication can have adverse effects on your health. It is important to follow the instructions provided by your healthcare provider or pharmacist and to ask questions if you are unsure about the dosage.

In addition to knowing the correct dosage, it is also important to be aware of the potential side effects of your medications. Some medications may cause drowsiness, dizziness, or other unwanted effects. By knowing what to expect, you can better manage any side effects that may arise.

Another important aspect of understanding your medications is knowing the possible interactions between them. Some medications may interact with each other, causing them to be less effective or potentially harmful. It is important to inform your healthcare provider about all the medications you are taking, including over-the-counter medications and supplements, so they can assess any potential interactions.

Creating a Medication Schedule: Consistency is Key

Taking medications on a consistent schedule is crucial for their effectiveness. Many medications need to be taken at specific times of the day or with food. By creating a medication schedule that works for you, you can ensure that you are taking your medications as prescribed.

There are several tips for creating a medication schedule that works for you. First, try to align your medication schedule with your daily routine. For example, if you always eat breakfast at 8 am, you can take your morning medications at the same time. This will help you remember to take your medications and make it easier to incorporate them into your daily routine.

Another tip is to use reminders. Set alarms on your phone or use a pill organizer with built-in reminders to help you remember to take your medications. You can also ask a family member or friend to remind you if needed.

Storing Medications Safely: Tips for Keeping Your Meds Secure and Accessible

Storing medications in a safe and secure location is important to prevent accidental ingestion by children or pets and to maintain their effectiveness. Medications should be stored in a cool, dry place away from direct sunlight and moisture. Avoid storing medications in the bathroom, as the humidity can degrade them.

It is also important to keep medications accessible and organized. This will make it easier for you to find and take your medications as prescribed. Consider using a pill organizer with compartments for each day of the week. This can help you keep track of which medications you have taken and which ones still need to be taken.

Communicating with Your Healthcare Provider: The Importance of Open Dialogue

Open communication with your healthcare provider is essential for effective medication management. Your healthcare provider needs to know about all the medications you are taking, including over-the-counter medications and supplements, in order to assess any potential interactions or side effects.

It is important to discuss any concerns or questions you may have about your medications with your healthcare provider. They can provide guidance and address any issues that may arise. If you are experiencing side effects or if your medication is not working as expected, it is important to inform your healthcare provider so they can make any necessary adjustments.

Tracking Your Medications: Tools and Apps to Help You Stay Organized

Tracking your medications can help you stay organized and ensure that you are taking them as prescribed. There are several tools and apps available that can help you track your medications.

One option is a pill organizer with compartments for each day of the week. This can help you keep track of which medications you have taken and which ones still need to be taken. Some pill organizers also have built-in reminders or alarms to help you remember to take your medications.

Another option is to use a medication tracking app on your smartphone or tablet. These apps allow you to input your medications and set reminders for when to take them. Some apps also provide information about potential side effects and interactions.

Refilling Prescriptions: Tips for Avoiding Delays and Running Out of Medications

Refilling prescriptions on time is crucial to avoid running out of medications. It is important to plan ahead and ensure that you have enough medication to last until your next refill.

One tip is to set reminders for when to refill your prescriptions. This can help you stay on top of your medication supply and avoid any delays. You can also ask your pharmacy if they offer automatic refills or prescription synchronization, where all your medications are refilled at the same time.

If you are traveling or unable to pick up your prescription in person, consider using a mail-order pharmacy or online pharmacy. These services can deliver your medications directly to your doorstep, ensuring that you have a continuous supply.

Managing Medications While Traveling: Planning Ahead for a Smooth Trip

Managing medications while traveling requires some planning ahead to ensure that you have an adequate supply and that they are stored properly. Here are some tips for managing medications while traveling:

- Pack enough medication for the duration of your trip, plus a few extra days in case of any delays.

- Keep your medications in their original containers with the labels intact, in case you need to show them at security checkpoints.

- If you are traveling internationally, check the regulations of the country you are visiting regarding medication importation. Some medications may be restricted or require additional documentation.

- If you are traveling to a different time zone, adjust your medication schedule accordingly. You can use a medication tracking app to help you stay on schedule.

- If you are flying, keep your medications in your carry-on bag to ensure that they are easily accessible and not subject to extreme temperatures in the cargo hold.

Dealing with Medication Costs: Finding Affordable Options and Assistance Programs

The cost of medications can be a barrier for many people. However, there are options available to help make medications more affordable.

One option is to ask your healthcare provider or pharmacist if there are generic versions of your medications available. Generic medications are often less expensive than brand-name medications and contain the same active ingredients.

Another option is to explore assistance programs for medication costs. Many pharmaceutical companies offer patient assistance programs that provide free or discounted medications to eligible individuals. You can also check if you qualify for any government assistance programs, such as Medicaid or Medicare.

Addressing Medication Adherence Challenges: Strategies for Staying Motivated and Compliant

Medication adherence can be challenging for many people, especially when taking multiple medications or dealing with complex dosing schedules. However, there are strategies that can help you stay motivated and compliant with your medication use.

One strategy is to set reminders for when to take your medications. This can be done using alarms on your phone, pill organizers with built-in reminders, or medication tracking apps.

Another strategy is to establish a routine. Taking your medications at the same time each day can help make it a habit and easier to remember.

If you are struggling with medication adherence, it is important to discuss this with your healthcare provider. They can provide guidance and support to help you overcome any challenges you may be facing.

Taking Control of Your Medication Management for Better Health

Taking control of your medication management is essential for maintaining good health. By understanding your medications, creating a medication schedule, storing medications safely, communicating with your healthcare provider, tracking your medications, refilling prescriptions on time, managing medications while traveling, addressing medication costs, and finding strategies for medication adherence, you can ensure that you are using your medications safely and effectively.

Proper medication use can have a significant impact on your overall health and well-being. By taking the necessary steps to manage your medications effectively, you can improve your quality of life and reduce the risk of complications from improper medication use. Remember to always consult with your healthcare provider or pharmacist if you have any questions or concerns about your medications.

Chapter 5: Chapter 5: Mastering Medication Management: Tips and Tricks for Staying on Track

Medication management plays a crucial role in maintaining good health. Whether you are taking prescription medications for a chronic condition or over-the-counter medications for occasional ailments, it is important to understand how to properly use and manage your medications. Improper medication use can lead to serious health risks and complications. By taking control of your medication management, you can ensure that you are using your medications safely and effectively.

Understanding Your Medications: Dosages, Side Effects, and Interactions

One of the key aspects of medication management is understanding your medications. This includes knowing the correct dosage of each medication you are taking. Taking too little or too much of a medication can have adverse effects on your health. It is important to follow the instructions provided by your healthcare provider or pharmacist and to ask questions if you are unsure about the dosage.

In addition to knowing the correct dosage, it is also important to be aware of the potential side effects of your medications. Some medications may cause drowsiness, dizziness, or other unwanted effects. By knowing what to expect, you can better manage any side effects that may arise.

Another important aspect of understanding your medications is knowing the possible interactions between them. Some medications may interact with each other, causing them to be less effective or potentially harmful. It is important to inform your healthcare provider about all the medications you are taking, including over-the-counter medications and supplements, so they can assess any potential interactions.

Creating a Medication Schedule: Consistency is Key

Taking medications on a consistent schedule is crucial for their effectiveness. Many medications need to be taken at specific times of the day or with food. By creating a medication schedule that works for you, you can ensure that you are taking your medications as prescribed.

There are several tips for creating a medication schedule that works for you. First, try to align your medication schedule with your daily routine. For example, if you always eat breakfast at 8 am, you can take your morning medications at the same time. This will help you remember to take your medications and make it easier to incorporate them into your daily routine.

Another tip is to use reminders. Set alarms on your phone or use a pill organizer with built-in reminders to help you remember to take your medications. You can also ask a family member or friend to remind you if needed.

Storing Medications Safely: Tips for Keeping Your Meds Secure and Accessible

Storing medications in a safe and secure location is important to prevent accidental ingestion by children or pets and to maintain their effectiveness. Medications should be stored in a cool, dry place away from direct sunlight and moisture. Avoid storing medications in the bathroom, as the humidity can degrade them.

It is also important to keep medications accessible and organized. This will make it easier for you to find and take your medications as prescribed. Consider using a pill organizer with compartments for each day of the week. This can help you keep track of which medications you have taken and which ones still need to be taken.

Communicating with Your Healthcare Provider: The Importance of Open Dialogue

Open communication with your healthcare provider is essential for effective medication management. Your healthcare provider needs to know about all the medications you are taking, including over-the-counter medications and supplements, in order to assess any potential interactions or side effects.

It is important to discuss any concerns or questions you may have about your medications with your healthcare provider. They can provide guidance and address any issues that may arise. If you are experiencing side effects or if your medication is not working as expected, it is important to inform your healthcare provider so they can make any necessary adjustments.

Tracking Your Medications: Tools and Apps to Help You Stay Organized

Tracking your medications can help you stay organized and ensure that you are taking them as prescribed. There are several tools and apps available that can help you track your medications.

One option is a pill organizer with compartments for each day of the week. This can help you keep track of which medications you have taken and which ones still need to be taken. Some pill organizers also have built-in reminders or alarms to help you remember to take your medications.

Another option is to use a medication tracking app on your smartphone or tablet. These apps allow you to input your medications and set reminders for when to take them. Some apps also provide information about potential side effects and interactions.

Refilling Prescriptions: Tips for Avoiding Delays and Running Out of Medications

Refilling prescriptions on time is crucial to avoid running out of medications. It is important to plan ahead and ensure that you have enough medication to last until your next refill.

One tip is to set reminders for when to refill your prescriptions. This can help you stay on top of your medication supply and avoid any delays. You can also ask your pharmacy if they offer automatic refills or prescription synchronization, where all your medications are refilled at the same time.

If you are traveling or unable to pick up your prescription in person, consider using a mail-order pharmacy or online pharmacy. These services can deliver your medications directly to your doorstep, ensuring that you have a continuous supply.

Managing Medications While Traveling: Planning Ahead for a Smooth Trip

Managing medications while traveling requires some planning ahead to ensure that you have an adequate supply and that they are stored properly. Here are some tips for managing medications while traveling:

- Pack enough medication for the duration of your trip, plus a few extra days in case of any delays.

- Keep your medications in their original containers with the labels intact, in case you need to show them at security checkpoints.

- If you are traveling internationally, check the regulations of the country you are visiting regarding medication importation. Some medications may be restricted or require additional documentation.

- If you are traveling to a different time zone, adjust your medication schedule accordingly. You can use a medication tracking app to help you stay on schedule.

- If you are flying, keep your medications in your carry-on bag to ensure that they are easily accessible and not subject to extreme temperatures in the cargo hold.

Dealing with Medication Costs: Finding Affordable Options and Assistance Programs

The cost of medications can be a barrier for many people. However, there are options available to help make medications more affordable.

One option is to ask your healthcare provider or pharmacist if there are generic versions of your medications available. Generic medications are often less expensive than brand-name medications and contain the same active ingredients.

Another option is to explore assistance programs for medication costs. Many pharmaceutical companies offer patient assistance programs that provide free or discounted medications to eligible individuals. You can also check if you qualify for any government assistance programs, such as Medicaid or Medicare.

Addressing Medication Adherence Challenges: Strategies for Staying Motivated and Compliant

Medication adherence can be challenging for many people, especially when taking multiple medications or dealing with complex dosing schedules. However, there are strategies that can help you stay motivated and compliant with your medication use.

One strategy is to set reminders for when to take your medications. This can be done using alarms on your phone, pill organizers with built-in reminders, or medication tracking apps.

Another strategy is to establish a routine. Taking your medications at the same time each day can help make it a habit and easier to remember.

If you are struggling with medication adherence, it is important to discuss this with your healthcare provider. They can provide guidance and support to help you overcome any challenges you may be facing.

Taking Control of Your Medication Management for Better Health

Taking control of your medication management is essential for maintaining good health. By understanding your medications, creating a medication schedule, storing medications safely, communicating with your healthcare provider, tracking your medications, refilling prescriptions on time, managing medications while traveling, addressing medication costs, and finding strategies for medication adherence, you can ensure that you are using your medications safely and effectively.

Proper medication use can have a significant impact on your overall health and well-being. By taking the necessary steps to manage your medications effectively, you can improve your quality of life and reduce the risk of complications from improper medication use. Remember to always consult with your healthcare provider or pharmacist if you have any questions or concerns about your medications.

Chapter 6: The Holistic Lifestyle: A Journey to Wellness and Self-Discovery

Living a holistic lifestyle has become increasingly popular in recent years as people seek to improve their overall well-being and find balance in their lives. Holistic living is an approach that focuses on the whole person - mind, body, and spirit - and emphasizes the interconnectedness of all aspects of life. It involves making conscious choices that promote health and well-being in all areas of life, including nutrition, exercise, relationships, and spirituality. By adopting a holistic lifestyle, individuals can experience improved physical health, mental clarity, emotional well-being, and spiritual growth.

Understanding the Concept of Holistic Lifestyle

A holistic lifestyle is an approach to living that recognizes the interconnectedness of all aspects of life and seeks to create balance and harmony in each area. It is based on the belief that each person is a whole being made up of various parts - physical, mental, emotional, and spiritual - and that these parts are all interconnected and influence one another. The principles of holistic living include taking a proactive approach to health and well-being, focusing on prevention rather than just treating symptoms, and recognizing the importance of self-care and self-awareness.

The Importance of Mind-Body Connection

The mind-body connection is the idea that our thoughts, emotions, beliefs, and attitudes can have a direct impact on our physical health. Research has shown that stress, for example, can lead to a variety of physical ailments such as headaches, digestive issues, and weakened immune function. On the other hand, positive emotions like joy and gratitude have been linked to improved immune function and overall well-being. By understanding and nurturing the mind-body connection, individuals can improve their overall health and well-being.

The Role of Nutrition in Holistic Living

Nutrition plays a crucial role in holistic living as it directly affects both the body and mind. A healthy diet provides the necessary nutrients for optimal physical health while also supporting mental clarity and emotional well-being. Eating a balanced diet that includes a variety of fruits, vegetables, whole grains, lean proteins, and healthy fats can help prevent chronic diseases, boost energy levels, improve mood, and support overall well-being. Additionally, mindful eating practices such as paying attention to hunger and fullness cues and savoring each bite can enhance the overall dining experience and promote a healthy relationship with food.

Benefits of Practicing Mindfulness and Meditation

Mindfulness and meditation are practices that can greatly enhance holistic living. Mindfulness involves being fully present in the moment and paying attention to one's thoughts, feelings, and sensations without judgment. Meditation is a practice that involves focusing one's attention and eliminating the stream of thoughts that often clutter the mind. Both practices have been shown to reduce stress, improve focus and concentration, enhance emotional well-being, and promote a sense of inner peace. By incorporating mindfulness and meditation into daily life, individuals can cultivate a greater sense of self-awareness, reduce stress levels, and improve overall well-being.

The Significance of Exercise in Holistic Wellness

Exercise is an essential component of holistic wellness as it benefits both the body and mind. Regular physical activity has been shown to improve cardiovascular health, strengthen muscles and bones, boost mood, reduce stress levels, improve sleep quality, and enhance cognitive function. Engaging in activities that you enjoy such as walking, dancing, swimming, or practicing yoga can make exercise more enjoyable and sustainable. By incorporating regular exercise into your routine, you can experience improved physical health, increased energy levels, enhanced mental clarity, and a greater sense of well-being.

Exploring Alternative Therapies for Holistic Healing

Alternative therapies are non-conventional approaches to healing that focus on treating the whole person rather than just the symptoms of a specific condition. These therapies can be used in conjunction with traditional medical treatments or as standalone practices. Examples of alternative therapies include acupuncture, chiropractic care, herbal medicine, energy healing, and aromatherapy. These therapies can help promote balance and harmony in the body, mind, and spirit and support overall well-being.

Nurturing Relationships for Holistic Growth

Healthy relationships are an important aspect of holistic growth as they provide support, connection, and a sense of belonging. Positive relationships can enhance overall well-being, reduce stress levels, improve self-esteem, and promote personal growth. It is important to cultivate healthy relationships by practicing effective communication, setting boundaries, and prioritizing quality time with loved ones. By nurturing relationships, individuals can experience greater happiness, fulfillment, and overall well-being.

The Impact of Environment on Holistic Lifestyle

The environment in which we live can have a significant impact on our health and well-being. A healthy environment includes clean air, clean water, access to nature, and a safe and supportive community. Creating a healthy environment involves making conscious choices that promote sustainability, reducing exposure to toxins, and surrounding oneself with positive influences. By creating a healthy environment, individuals can support their holistic lifestyle and enhance their overall well-being.

Overcoming Challenges in Holistic Living

Living a holistic lifestyle can come with its own set of challenges. Some common challenges include finding time for self-care, maintaining healthy habits in the face of societal pressures, and overcoming resistance to change. To overcome these challenges, it is important to prioritize self-care and make it a non-negotiable part of your routine. It can also be helpful to seek support from like-minded individuals or join a community that shares your values. By acknowledging and addressing these challenges head-on, individuals can overcome obstacles and continue on their journey towards holistic living.

Embracing Spirituality for Holistic Transformation

Spirituality is an integral part of holistic living as it involves connecting with something greater than oneself and finding meaning and purpose in life. Spirituality can take many forms and can be practiced through religious beliefs, meditation, prayer, or engaging in activities that bring joy and fulfillment. By embracing spirituality, individuals can experience a sense of inner peace, find guidance and support, and cultivate a deeper connection with themselves and the world around them.

The Journey to Self-Discovery through Holistic Lifestyle

Living a holistic lifestyle can be a transformative journey that leads to self-discovery and personal growth. By taking a holistic approach to life, individuals can gain a deeper understanding of themselves, their values, and their purpose. This journey involves self-reflection, self-care, and a commitment to personal growth. It may also involve exploring new practices, trying new experiences, and stepping outside of one's comfort zone. By embarking on this journey, individuals can discover their true potential and create a life that is aligned with their values and aspirations.

In conclusion, living a holistic lifestyle is about recognizing the interconnectedness of all aspects of life and making conscious choices that promote health and well-being in each area. By focusing on the mind, body, and spirit, individuals can experience improved physical health, mental clarity, emotional well-being, and spiritual growth. Incorporating practices such as mindfulness, healthy eating, regular exercise, nurturing relationships, and embracing spirituality can greatly enhance holistic living. It is never too late to start incorporating holistic practices into daily life and experience the transformative power of living in balance and harmony.

Chapter 7: Why Family Support is Crucial for Mental Health

Mental health is a crucial aspect of overall well-being. It affects how we think, feel, and act, and it plays a significant role in our ability to handle stress, relate to others, and make choices. Mental health disorders, such as depression, anxiety, and bipolar disorder, affect millions of people worldwide. These conditions can have a profound impact on individuals and their families. That's why family support is so important in mental health recovery and wellness.

Understanding Mental Health and Its Impact on Individuals and Families

Mental health issues can have a significant impact on families and relationships. When a family member is struggling with a mental health disorder, it can create tension, stress, and conflict within the family unit. The individual may experience feelings of isolation, shame, and guilt, which can further exacerbate their mental health issues. Family members may also feel overwhelmed, helpless, or unsure of how to support their loved one.

The Role of Family Support in Mental Health Recovery

Family support can provide emotional and practical support to individuals with mental health issues. By offering a listening ear, empathy, and understanding, family members can create a safe space for their loved one to express their feelings and concerns. This emotional support can help individuals feel less alone and isolated in their struggles.

In addition to emotional support, family members can also provide practical assistance in managing mental health issues. This may include helping with medication management, accompanying the individual to therapy appointments, or assisting with daily tasks when needed. By offering this practical support, family members can help alleviate some of the burdens that come with managing a mental health disorder.

Building Strong Family Relationships: A Key to Mental Health Support

Strong family relationships are essential for mental health support. When family members have open lines of communication, trust each other, and show empathy towards one another, they create a foundation for support and understanding. Building strong family relationships requires ongoing effort and commitment from all members.

Communication is a vital component of building strong family relationships. It involves actively listening to one another, expressing thoughts and feelings honestly and respectfully, and being open to different perspectives. By fostering open and honest communication, family members can better understand each other's needs and provide the necessary support.

Trust is another crucial element of strong family relationships. Trust is built over time through consistent actions, honesty, and reliability. When family members trust each other, they feel safe and secure in sharing their vulnerabilities and seeking support when needed.

Empathy is the ability to understand and share the feelings of another person. It is an essential quality in building strong family relationships. By practicing empathy, family members can better understand the experiences and emotions of their loved ones with mental health issues. This understanding can help create a supportive and non-judgmental environment.

How Family Support Can Help Prevent Mental Health Issues

Family support can also play a role in preventing mental health issues. By promoting healthy coping mechanisms and stress management techniques, families can help individuals develop resilience and better manage life's challenges. Family members can model healthy behaviors, such as engaging in regular exercise, practicing mindfulness, and seeking social support when needed.

In addition to promoting healthy coping mechanisms, family support can also help individuals recognize and address mental health issues early on. By being aware of the signs and symptoms of mental health disorders, family members can encourage their loved ones to seek professional help when necessary. Early intervention is crucial in preventing mental health issues from worsening or becoming chronic.

The Benefits of Family Therapy for Mental Health Treatment

Family therapy is a form of therapy that involves the entire family unit in the treatment process. It can be beneficial for individuals with mental health issues and their families by helping them work through challenges together. Family therapy provides a safe space for open communication, conflict resolution, and problem-solving.

One of the primary benefits of family therapy is improved communication. Family members learn effective communication skills, such as active listening and expressing thoughts and feelings in a non-confrontational manner. These skills can help reduce conflict and promote understanding and empathy within the family.

Family therapy also helps families develop strategies for managing the challenges that come with mental health issues. Therapists can provide education about mental health disorders, teach coping skills, and offer guidance on how to support their loved ones effectively. By working together as a team, families can create a supportive environment that fosters mental health recovery and wellness.

Overcoming Stigma: How Family Support Can Help Break Down Mental Health Barriers

Stigma surrounding mental health can prevent individuals from seeking help. It can create feelings of shame, embarrassment, and fear of judgment. Family support plays a crucial role in breaking down these barriers by promoting understanding and acceptance.

When family members are educated about mental health disorders and their impact, they can challenge misconceptions and stereotypes. By openly discussing mental health within the family, they create an environment where individuals feel safe to seek help without fear of judgment or stigma.

Family members can also serve as advocates for their loved ones with mental health issues. They can speak out against discrimination, educate others about mental health, and support policies that promote access to mental health care. By actively challenging stigma, families can help create a more inclusive and supportive society for individuals with mental health issues.

Supporting Children and Adolescents with Mental Health Challenges: The Role of Family

Children and adolescents with mental health challenges often rely on their families for support. Family support is crucial in helping them feel safe, secure, and understood. It is essential for parents and caregivers to create an environment where children feel comfortable expressing their thoughts and emotions without fear of judgment or punishment.

Family members can provide emotional support by actively listening to their children's concerns, validating their feelings, and offering reassurance. They can also help children develop healthy coping mechanisms and stress management techniques. By teaching children these skills, families can empower them to navigate life's challenges and build resilience.

In addition to emotional support, families can also play a role in advocating for their children's mental health needs. This may involve working with schools, healthcare providers, and other professionals to ensure that children receive the necessary support and accommodations. By being actively involved in their children's mental health care, families can help set them up for success.

The Importance of Communication and Active Listening in Family Mental Health Support

Communication and active listening are essential components of family mental health support. Effective communication involves expressing thoughts and feelings honestly and respectfully, while active listening requires giving full attention to the speaker and seeking to understand their perspective.

When family members communicate openly and honestly, they create an environment where individuals feel safe to express their thoughts and emotions. This open communication can help prevent misunderstandings, reduce conflict, and promote understanding within the family.

Active listening is equally important in family mental health support. It involves giving full attention to the speaker, maintaining eye contact, and providing verbal and non-verbal cues that show understanding and empathy. By actively listening to their loved ones with mental health issues, family members can better understand their experiences and provide the necessary support.

Supporting Family Members with Mental Health Issues: Self-Care and Coping Strategies

Supporting family members with mental health issues can be challenging and emotionally taxing. It is essential for family members to prioritize their own self-care and coping strategies to maintain their own mental health and well-being.

Self-care involves engaging in activities that promote relaxation, stress reduction, and overall well-being. This may include exercise, practicing mindfulness or meditation, spending time in nature, or engaging in hobbies or activities that bring joy. By taking care of themselves, family members can better support their loved ones with mental health issues.

Coping strategies are also essential for family members to manage the stress and challenges that come with supporting someone with a mental health disorder. This may involve seeking support from friends or support groups, attending therapy or counseling, or practicing stress management techniques such as deep breathing or journaling. By developing healthy coping strategies, family members can better navigate the ups and downs of supporting their loved ones.

The Power of Family Support in Mental Health Recovery and Wellness

Family support is a crucial component of mental health recovery and wellness. By building strong family relationships, promoting understanding and acceptance, and providing emotional and practical support, families can help individuals with mental health issues thrive. Through open communication, active listening, and empathy, families can create a safe and supportive environment where individuals feel understood and valued. By prioritizing self-care and coping strategies, family members can maintain their own mental health and well-being while supporting their loved ones. Together, families can play a significant role in promoting mental health recovery and wellness for all.

Chapter 8: From Shame to Strength: Embracing Your Identity and Fighting Stigma

Stigma is a powerful force that can have a profound impact on individuals and communities. It is a social phenomenon that involves the labeling and devaluation of certain groups or individuals based on characteristics or behaviors that are perceived as deviant or undesirable. Stigma can manifest in various forms, such as discrimination, prejudice, and stereotypes, and it can have far-reaching consequences for those who experience it.

The impact of stigma goes beyond the individual level and extends to the broader community. Stigmatized individuals may face barriers to accessing healthcare, education, employment, and social support. They may also experience higher rates of mental health issues, substance abuse, and social isolation. Stigma can perpetuate inequality and marginalization, creating a cycle of disadvantage that is difficult to break.

Understanding the Impact of Stigma on Identity

Identity is a complex concept that encompasses various aspects of an individual's sense of self, including their beliefs, values, experiences, and social roles. Stigma can have a profound impact on one's identity, leading to self-doubt, shame, and isolation.

When individuals are stigmatized, they may internalize the negative beliefs and stereotypes associated with their identity. This can lead to feelings of self-doubt and shame, as they begin to question their worth and value as a person. Stigma can erode one's sense of self-esteem and self-worth, making it difficult to maintain a positive sense of identity.

Stigma can also lead to social isolation and exclusion. Individuals who are stigmatized may face rejection from their peers, family members, or community members. This can result in feelings of loneliness and alienation, further exacerbating the negative impact on their identity.

The Power of Self-Acceptance in Overcoming Shame

Self-acceptance is a crucial component in overcoming shame and building resilience in the face of stigma. It involves recognizing and embracing all aspects of oneself, including the parts that may be stigmatized or marginalized.

Practicing self-compassion and self-love is essential in cultivating self-acceptance. This involves treating oneself with kindness and understanding, rather than judgment and criticism. It means acknowledging that everyone has flaws and imperfections, and that these do not define one's worth as a person.

Strategies for practicing self-compassion and self-love include engaging in positive self-talk, practicing mindfulness and meditation, seeking therapy or counseling, and surrounding oneself with supportive and affirming people. It is important to challenge negative self-beliefs and replace them with positive affirmations.

Finding Support: Building a Network of Allies

Having a support system is crucial in overcoming stigma and building resilience. Allies are individuals who are supportive, understanding, and willing to stand up against stigma and discrimination. They can provide emotional support, validation, and advocacy.

Building a network of allies starts with reaching out to trusted friends, family members, or community members who are accepting and non-judgmental. It is important to communicate one's needs and experiences openly and honestly, as this can help foster understanding and empathy.

Finding safe spaces is also essential in building a support system. Safe spaces are environments where individuals can feel accepted, understood, and valued without fear of judgment or discrimination. These spaces can be physical locations, such as community centers or support groups, or virtual spaces, such as online forums or social media groups.

Challenging Stereotypes: Advocating for Yourself and Others

Challenging stereotypes is an important step in overcoming stigma and promoting understanding. Stereotypes are oversimplified beliefs or assumptions about a particular group of people based on their characteristics or behaviors. They can perpetuate stigma by reinforcing negative beliefs and perpetuating discrimination.

Advocating for yourself and others involves speaking up against stereotypes and challenging discriminatory attitudes and behaviors. This can be done through education and awareness-raising, sharing personal stories and experiences, and engaging in dialogue with others.

It is important to remember that advocacy does not have to be confrontational or aggressive. It can involve having open and respectful conversations with others, sharing information and resources, and promoting empathy and understanding.

The Role of Education in Fighting Stigma

Education plays a crucial role in reducing stigma and promoting understanding. By providing accurate information and dispelling myths and misconceptions, education can challenge stereotypes and promote empathy and acceptance.

Educational initiatives can take various forms, such as workshops, trainings, public awareness campaigns, and curriculum development. These initiatives can target different audiences, including students, healthcare professionals, employers, and community members.

Resources for education on stigma can include books, articles, documentaries, podcasts, and online courses. It is important to seek out diverse perspectives and voices to gain a comprehensive understanding of the issues at hand.

The Importance of Language: Using Inclusive Terminology

Language plays a powerful role in shaping perceptions and attitudes towards stigmatized groups. Inclusive language is language that respects and includes all individuals, regardless of their characteristics or identities. It avoids using derogatory or offensive terms and promotes respect and dignity.

Using inclusive language is important in reducing stigma because it challenges stereotypes and promotes equality. It acknowledges the diversity of human experiences and identities and recognizes the inherent worth and value of all individuals.

Examples of inclusive language include using person-first language (e.g., "person with a disability" instead of "disabled person"), avoiding derogatory terms or slurs, using gender-neutral language when appropriate, and being mindful of the impact of words on others.

Addressing Internalized Stigma: Overcoming Self-Doubt and Fear

Internalized stigma refers to the internalization of negative beliefs and stereotypes about oneself. It occurs when individuals begin to believe and internalize the negative messages they receive from society, leading to self-doubt, fear, and self-criticism.

Overcoming internalized stigma involves challenging these negative beliefs and replacing them with positive and affirming ones. This can be done through therapy or counseling, self-reflection and introspection, and engaging in activities that promote self-esteem and self-worth.

It is important to remember that overcoming internalized stigma is a process that takes time and effort. It requires patience, self-compassion, and a willingness to challenge deeply ingrained beliefs and thought patterns.

Coping with Discrimination: Strategies for Resilience

Discrimination is a form of stigma that involves the unfair treatment or exclusion of individuals based on their characteristics or identities. Coping with discrimination requires resilience and the ability to navigate challenging situations while maintaining one's sense of self-worth and dignity.

Strategies for coping with discrimination include seeking support from allies and support networks, engaging in self-care activities, practicing assertiveness and boundary-setting, and seeking legal recourse when appropriate.

Self-care is particularly important in coping with discrimination, as it helps individuals maintain their physical, emotional, and mental well-being. This can involve engaging in activities that bring joy and relaxation, such as exercise, hobbies, or spending time with loved ones.

Celebrating Diversity: Embracing Differences and Finding Strength in Community

Celebrating diversity is an important step in reducing stigma and promoting inclusivity. It involves recognizing and valuing the unique characteristics, experiences, and perspectives of individuals from different backgrounds.

Embracing differences can bring strength to communities by fostering creativity, innovation, and collaboration. It can lead to a more inclusive society where everyone feels valued and respected for who they are.

Examples of celebrating diversity include organizing cultural events or festivals, promoting diversity in media representation, supporting diverse businesses or organizations, and engaging in intercultural dialogue.

The Role of Media in Shaping Perceptions and Challenging Stigma

Media plays a powerful role in shaping perceptions and attitudes towards stigmatized groups. It can either perpetuate stigma by reinforcing stereotypes and negative beliefs or challenge stigma by promoting empathy, understanding, and inclusivity.

Media initiatives that challenge stigma can include films, documentaries, TV shows, news articles, and social media campaigns that highlight the experiences and perspectives of stigmatized individuals. These initiatives can help humanize and destigmatize certain groups, promoting empathy and understanding.

Consumers of media also have a role to play in challenging stigma. By supporting diverse and inclusive media content, engaging in critical analysis of media messages, and sharing positive and affirming stories, individuals can contribute to the reduction of stigma.

Moving Forward: Empowering Yourself and Others to Create Change

Creating change and reducing stigma requires action at both the individual and collective levels. Empowering oneself and others involves taking steps to challenge stigma, promote understanding, and advocate for equality.

Strategies for empowering oneself and others include educating oneself on the issues at hand, engaging in dialogue with others, sharing personal stories and experiences, supporting organizations or initiatives that promote inclusivity, and using one's voice to speak up against discrimination.

It is important to remember that change takes time and effort. It requires persistence, resilience, and a commitment to challenging the status quo. By taking small steps towards creating change in our own lives and communities, we can contribute to a more inclusive and accepting society.

Stigma is a powerful force that can have a profound impact on individuals and communities. It can lead to self-doubt, shame, isolation, discrimination, and inequality. However, by understanding the impact of stigma on identity, practicing self-acceptance, building a network of allies, challenging stereotypes, promoting education, using inclusive language, addressing internalized stigma, coping with discrimination, celebrating diversity, challenging media representations, and empowering oneself and others to create change, we can work towards reducing stigma and promoting understanding.

It is important for each of us to take steps towards reducing stigma in our own lives and communities. This can involve educating ourselves, challenging our own biases and assumptions, speaking up against discrimination, supporting organizations or initiatives that promote inclusivity, and using our voices to advocate for equality. By working together, we can create a more inclusive and accepting society where everyone feels valued and respected for who they are.

Chapter 9: Breaking the Stigma: Sharing My Recovery Story

Mental illness is a prevalent issue that affects millions of people worldwide. Despite its prevalence, there is still a negative stigma surrounding mental health that prevents many individuals from seeking the help they need. This stigma can lead to feelings of shame, fear, and isolation, making it even more difficult for those struggling with mental illness to reach out for support.

Breaking the stigma around mental health is crucial because it can save lives. When individuals feel comfortable seeking help and talking openly about their struggles, they are more likely to receive the support and treatment they need. By breaking the stigma, we can create a society that is more understanding, compassionate, and supportive of those with mental illness.

My Struggle with Mental Illness: A Personal Account

I have personally experienced the challenges of living with mental illness. For years, I battled with depression and anxiety, but I was too ashamed to seek help. I felt like I was weak or broken for not being able to handle my emotions on my own. This stigma surrounding mental health prevented me from reaching out for support and caused me to suffer in silence.

My mental illness had a significant impact on my daily life and relationships. I found it difficult to concentrate at work, often feeling overwhelmed and unable to complete tasks. My relationships suffered as well because I was constantly on edge and irritable. I isolated myself from friends and family, believing that they wouldn't understand or accept me if they knew about my struggles.

The Impact of Stigma on Seeking Help

Stigma can have a profound impact on an individual's decision to seek help for their mental health issues. The fear of being judged or labeled as "crazy" can be paralyzing, causing individuals to suffer in silence rather than reaching out for support. The shame associated with mental illness can make individuals feel like they are weak or flawed, further perpetuating the stigma.

The negative stigma surrounding mental health can also lead to a lack of understanding and empathy from others. People may dismiss or downplay the severity of mental illness, making it even more difficult for individuals to seek help. This lack of support and understanding can exacerbate feelings of isolation and make it harder for individuals to recover.

Overcoming Shame and Fear: The First Steps to Recovery

Overcoming shame and fear is an essential first step in the recovery journey. It's important to remember that mental illness is not a personal failing or weakness, but a medical condition that can be treated. Practicing self-compassion and self-care is crucial in breaking through the shame and fear associated with mental illness.

One way to overcome shame and fear is by educating yourself about mental health. Understanding that mental illness is a common and treatable condition can help reduce feelings of shame and isolation. Surrounding yourself with supportive and understanding individuals can also make a significant difference in overcoming shame and fear.

The Role of Therapy and Medication in My Recovery Journey

Therapy and medication have played a crucial role in my recovery journey. Therapy provided me with a safe space to explore my thoughts and emotions, helping me gain insight into my struggles. It allowed me to develop coping mechanisms and strategies to manage my mental health effectively.

Medication also played a vital role in my recovery. It helped stabilize my mood and reduce the intensity of my symptoms, allowing me to function more effectively in my daily life. Finding the right combination of therapy and medication may take time, but it is worth the effort in order to find what works best for you.

Building a Support System: The Importance of Friends and Family

Having a support system is essential when dealing with mental illness. Friends and family can provide emotional support, understanding, and encouragement during difficult times. They can be a source of comfort and reassurance, helping to alleviate feelings of isolation and loneliness.

Building a support system starts with open and honest communication. Sharing your struggles with trusted friends and family members can help them understand what you're going through and provide the support you need. It's important to surround yourself with individuals who are empathetic, non-judgmental, and willing to listen.

Finding Purpose and Meaning in Life After Mental Illness

Finding purpose and meaning in life after mental illness can be a challenging journey. Mental illness can often strip away our sense of identity and leave us feeling lost and disconnected. However, it is possible to rebuild a sense of purpose and find meaning in life again.

One way to find purpose is by exploring your passions and interests. Engaging in activities that bring you joy and fulfillment can help you regain a sense of purpose. Setting goals and working towards them can also provide a sense of direction and meaning.

Challenging Negative Self-Talk and Building Self-Esteem

Negative self-talk can be incredibly damaging to our mental health. It reinforces feelings of shame, fear, and inadequacy, making it even more difficult to recover from mental illness. Challenging negative self-talk is crucial in building self-esteem and promoting positive mental health.

One way to challenge negative self-talk is by practicing self-compassion. Treat yourself with kindness and understanding, just as you would treat a loved one. Remind yourself that you are not defined by your mental illness and that you are deserving of love and acceptance.

Coping Strategies for Managing Triggers and Relapses

Managing triggers and preventing relapses is an ongoing process in the recovery journey. Developing coping strategies can help individuals navigate difficult situations and prevent setbacks in their mental health.

One coping strategy is practicing self-awareness. Pay attention to your thoughts, emotions, and physical sensations, as they can provide valuable insight into your triggers. Engaging in self-care activities, such as exercise, meditation, and journaling, can also help manage stress and prevent relapses.

Advocating for Mental Health: How Sharing My

Story Can Help Others

Advocating for mental health is crucial in breaking the stigma and creating a more supportive society. Sharing your story can help others feel less alone and encourage them to seek help. It can also help educate others about mental illness and promote understanding and empathy.

Sharing your story can be done in various ways, such as writing articles, speaking at events, or participating in support groups. It's important to remember that sharing your story is a personal choice and should only be done when you feel comfortable and ready.

Breaking the Stigma, One Story at a Time.

Breaking the stigma around mental health is a collective effort that requires compassion, understanding, and open dialogue. By sharing our stories and advocating for mental health, we can create a society that supports and empowers individuals with mental illness. Together, we can break the stigma and ensure that everyone has access to the help they need.

Chapter 10: The Benefits of Being Self-Aware: Improving Your Relationships and Life Satisfaction

Self-awareness is a fundamental aspect of personal growth and success. It involves having a clear understanding of one's own thoughts, emotions, and behaviors, as well as how they impact oneself and others. By developing self-awareness, individuals can gain valuable insights into their strengths, weaknesses, and areas for improvement. This article will explore the various ways in which self-awareness can contribute to personal growth and success in different aspects of life.

Understanding Self-Awareness: A Key to Personal Growth

Self-awareness can be defined as the ability to objectively observe and understand one's own thoughts, emotions, and behaviors. It involves being conscious of one's strengths, weaknesses, values, and beliefs. Self-awareness is crucial for personal growth because it allows individuals to identify areas where they can improve and make positive changes.

When individuals are self-aware, they are better able to recognize their own patterns of behavior and thought. This awareness enables them to take responsibility for their actions and make conscious choices that align with their values and goals. By understanding their own strengths and weaknesses, individuals can focus on developing their strengths and addressing areas for improvement.

For example, someone who is self-aware may realize that they have a tendency to procrastinate when faced with challenging tasks. With this awareness, they can develop strategies to overcome procrastination and improve their productivity. Similarly, someone who is self-aware may recognize that they have a tendency to be overly critical of themselves. With this awareness, they can work on cultivating self-compassion and practicing self-care.

The Link Between Self-Awareness and Emotional Intelligence

Emotional intelligence refers to the ability to recognize, understand, and manage one's own emotions as well as the emotions of others. It involves skills such as empathy, self-regulation, and effective communication. Self-awareness is a key component of emotional intelligence because it allows individuals to accurately perceive and understand their own emotions.

When individuals are self-aware, they are better able to recognize and understand their own emotions. This awareness enables them to effectively manage their emotions and respond to situations in a more constructive manner. For example, someone who is self-aware may notice that they tend to become angry or defensive when receiving feedback. With this awareness, they can practice self-regulation techniques such as deep breathing or taking a pause before responding.

Furthermore, self-awareness allows individuals to have a better understanding of how their emotions impact their interactions with others. This understanding enables them to empathize with others and respond in a more compassionate and effective way. For example, someone who is self-aware may realize that they often feel anxious in social situations. With this awareness, they can be more understanding and supportive of others who may also be experiencing anxiety.

Self-Awareness: The Foundation of Healthy Relationships

Self-awareness plays a crucial role in building and maintaining healthy relationships. When individuals are self-aware, they are better able to understand their own needs, boundaries, and communication styles. This understanding allows them to effectively communicate their needs and establish healthy boundaries in relationships.

Additionally, self-awareness enables individuals to empathize with others and understand their perspectives. This empathy fosters better communication and deeper connections in relationships. For example, someone who is self-aware may recognize that they have a tendency to interrupt others during conversations. With this awareness, they can make a conscious effort to listen actively and give others the space to express themselves.

Furthermore, self-awareness allows individuals to take responsibility for their own actions and behaviors in relationships. This accountability promotes healthier dynamics and prevents the blame game. For example, someone who is self-aware may realize that they have a tendency to be passive-aggressive when feeling upset. With this awareness, they can work on expressing their feelings directly and assertively.

The Benefits of Self-Awareness for Career Success

Self-awareness is also crucial for career success. When individuals are self-aware, they have a clear understanding of their strengths, weaknesses, and areas for improvement. This understanding allows them to make informed decisions about their career path and set realistic goals.

Furthermore, self-awareness enables individuals to effectively manage their emotions and reactions in the workplace. This emotional intelligence is highly valued by employers and can contribute to better job performance and satisfaction. For example, someone who is self-aware may recognize that they tend to become easily overwhelmed in high-pressure situations. With this awareness, they can develop stress management techniques and seek support when needed.

Moreover, self-awareness allows individuals to identify their values and align them with their career choices. When individuals are aware of their values, they can make choices that are in line with their personal beliefs and priorities. This alignment leads to greater job satisfaction and fulfillment. For example, someone who is self-aware may realize that they value work-life balance and prioritize spending time with family. With this awareness, they can make career choices that allow for flexibility and prioritize their personal life.

How Self-Awareness Can Help You Manage Stress and Anxiety

Self-awareness is a powerful tool for managing stress and anxiety. When individuals are self-aware, they are better able to recognize the signs of stress and anxiety in their bodies and minds. This awareness allows them to take proactive steps to manage these emotions and prevent them from escalating.

For example, someone who is self-aware may notice that they experience tension in their shoulders or have racing thoughts when feeling stressed. With this awareness, they can practice relaxation techniques such as deep breathing or progressive muscle relaxation to alleviate the physical symptoms of stress.

Additionally, self-awareness enables individuals to identify the triggers or underlying causes of their stress and anxiety. This understanding allows them to address these root causes and develop healthier coping mechanisms. For example, someone who is self-aware may realize that they feel anxious when they have a lot of unfinished tasks. With this awareness, they can prioritize their tasks, break them down into smaller, manageable steps, and practice time management techniques.

Moreover, self-awareness allows individuals to recognize unhelpful thought patterns or beliefs that contribute to their stress and anxiety.

This awareness enables them to challenge and reframe these thoughts, leading to a more positive and balanced mindset. For example, someone who is self-aware may notice that they have a tendency to catastrophize or jump to worst-case scenarios. With this awareness, they can practice cognitive restructuring techniques and focus on more realistic and helpful thoughts.

The Importance of Self-Awareness in Decision-Making

Self-awareness is essential for making informed and rational decisions. When individuals are self-aware, they are better able to recognize their own biases, assumptions, and emotions that may influence their decision-making process. This awareness allows them to approach decisions with a more objective and rational mindset.

For example, someone who is self-aware may realize that they have a tendency to make impulsive decisions when feeling stressed or overwhelmed. With this awareness, they can practice decision-making techniques such as taking a step back, gathering more information, and considering the long-term consequences before making a decision.

Additionally, self-awareness enables individuals to identify their values and priorities when making decisions. This understanding allows them to make choices that align with their personal beliefs and goals. For example, someone who is self-aware may recognize that they value environmental sustainability and prioritize purchasing products from eco-friendly companies. With this awareness, they can make purchasing decisions that align with their values.

Moreover, self-awareness allows individuals to consider different perspectives and gather input from others when making decisions. This openness to feedback and collaboration leads to more well-rounded and informed decisions. For example, someone who is self-aware may realize that they have a tendency to dismiss others' opinions or ideas.

With this awareness, they can actively seek out diverse perspectives and engage in constructive dialogue before making a decision.

How to Develop Self-Awareness: Tips and Techniques

Developing self-awareness is an ongoing process that requires practice and reflection. Here are some tips and techniques for cultivating self-awareness:

1. Mindfulness: Mindfulness involves paying attention to the present moment without judgment. By practicing mindfulness, individuals can develop a greater awareness of their thoughts, emotions, and bodily sensations.

2. Journaling: Writing in a journal can help individuals reflect on their thoughts, emotions, and experiences. It provides a space for self-expression and self-reflection.

3. Seeking feedback: Asking for feedback from trusted friends, family members, or colleagues can provide valuable insights into one's strengths, weaknesses, and blind spots.

4. Self-reflection exercises: Engaging in self-reflection exercises such as asking oneself thought-provoking questions or completing personality assessments can help individuals gain a deeper understanding of themselves.

5. Therapy or coaching: Working with a therapist or coach can provide guidance and support in developing self-awareness. These professionals can help individuals explore their thoughts, emotions, and behaviors in a safe and non-judgmental environment.

It is important to note that developing self-awareness is an ongoing journey that requires consistency and commitment. It is not something that can be achieved overnight, but rather a lifelong practice.

The Role of Self-Awareness in Building Resilience

Self-awareness plays a crucial role in building resilience, which is the ability to bounce back from adversity and overcome challenges. When individuals are self-aware, they are better able to recognize their own strengths, resources, and coping mechanisms.

Furthermore, self-awareness allows individuals to identify their own triggers or stressors that may contribute to their challenges. This understanding enables them to develop strategies to manage these triggers and build resilience. For example, someone who is self-aware may realize that they feel overwhelmed when they have too many commitments. With this awareness, they can practice time management techniques and learn to say no when necessary.

Moreover, self-awareness enables individuals to recognize their own patterns of thinking and behavior that may hinder their resilience. This awareness allows them to challenge and reframe these patterns, leading to a more positive and adaptive mindset. For example, someone who is self-aware may notice that they have a tendency to catastrophize or think in all-or-nothing terms when facing challenges. With this awareness, they can practice cognitive restructuring techniques and focus on more realistic and helpful thoughts.

Additionally, self-awareness allows individuals to identify their own strengths and resources that can support their resilience. This understanding enables them to leverage these strengths and resources during challenging times. For example, someone who is self-aware may recognize that they have a strong support system of friends and family. With this awareness, they can reach out for support and lean on their loved ones during difficult times.

Self-Awareness and Mindfulness: A Powerful Combination

Self-awareness and mindfulness are closely intertwined and can work together to improve mental health and well-being. Mindfulness involves paying attention to the present moment without judgment, while self-awareness involves having a clear understanding of one's own thoughts, emotions, and behaviors.

By practicing mindfulness, individuals can develop a greater awareness of their thoughts, emotions, and bodily sensations. This awareness allows them to observe their experiences without getting caught up in them or reacting impulsively. For example, someone who is practicing mindfulness may notice that they are feeling anxious or stressed. With this awareness, they can choose to respond to these emotions in a more constructive way, such as practicing deep breathing or engaging in a calming activity.

Furthermore, self-awareness can enhance mindfulness by providing individuals with insights into their own patterns of thinking and behavior. This understanding allows them to approach mindfulness practice with a more open and curious mindset. For example, someone who is self-aware may notice that they have a tendency to judge themselves or others during mindfulness practice. With this awareness, they can practice self-compassion and cultivate a non-judgmental attitude.

Moreover, the combination of self-awareness and mindfulness can improve overall mental health and well-being. By developing self-awareness, individuals can gain insights into their own needs, values, and priorities. By practicing mindfulness, individuals can cultivate a greater sense of presence, acceptance, and gratitude. Together, these practices can lead to greater self-acceptance, reduced stress and anxiety, and improved overall well-being.

How Self-Awareness Can Help You Overcome Limiting Beliefs

Self-awareness is a powerful tool for identifying and overcoming limiting beliefs. Limiting beliefs are negative or self-defeating thoughts or beliefs that hold individuals back from reaching their full potential. When individuals are self-aware, they are better able to recognize these limiting beliefs and challenge them.

By developing self-awareness, individuals can gain insights into their own patterns of thinking and behavior. This awareness allows them to identify recurring negative thoughts or beliefs that may be holding them back. For example, someone who is self-aware may notice that they often think "I'm not good enough" or "I'll never succeed." With this awareness, they can challenge these thoughts and replace them with more positive and empowering beliefs.

Furthermore, self-awareness enables individuals to understand the origins of their limiting beliefs. This understanding allows them to explore the underlying reasons or experiences that have contributed to these beliefs. For example, someone who is self-aware may realize that their fear of failure stems from a childhood experience where they were criticized for making mistakes. With this awareness, they can work on healing these past wounds and reframing their beliefs about failure.

Moreover, self-awareness allows individuals to develop strategies for overcoming their limiting beliefs. This awareness enables them to identify their own strengths, resources, and coping mechanisms that can support their growth and success. For example, someone who is self-aware may recognize that they have a strong support system of friends and family who believe in them. With this awareness, they can seek support and encouragement from their loved ones when facing challenges.

The Long-Term Benefits of Self-Awareness for

Life Satisfaction

Self-awareness has numerous long-term benefits for life satisfaction and overall well-being. By developing self-awareness, individuals can gain a deeper understanding of themselves, their values, and their goals. This understanding allows them to make choices and live a life that is aligned with their authentic selves.

Furthermore, self-awareness enables individuals to cultivate self-acceptance and self-compassion. This acceptance and compassion lead to greater self-esteem and self-worth. For example, someone who is self-aware may recognize that they have a tendency to be overly critical of themselves. With this awareness, they can practice self-compassion and treat themselves with kindness and understanding.

Moreover, self-awareness allows individuals to develop healthier coping mechanisms for dealing with challenges and setbacks. This awareness enables them to recognize their own patterns of thinking and behavior that may hinder their growth or well-being. For example, someone who is self-aware may notice that they have a tendency to avoid difficult conversations or conflict. With this awareness, they can practice assertiveness skills and engage in open and honest communication.

Additionally, self care is important for maintaining good mental health. Taking time for oneself and engaging in activities that bring joy and relaxation can help reduce stress and prevent burnout. This can include practicing mindfulness or meditation, engaging in hobbies or creative outlets, and prioritizing self-care routines such as exercise, healthy eating, and getting enough sleep. By taking care of oneself, individuals can better manage their emotions, improve their overall well-being, and build resilience to cope with life's challenges.

Chapter 11: 10 Surprising Ways to Manage Your Symptoms Like a Pro!

Living with symptoms can have a significant impact on daily life. Whether it's chronic pain, fatigue, anxiety, or any other symptom, these experiences can make it difficult to function and enjoy life to the fullest. That's why managing symptoms is crucial for overall well-being. By finding effective ways to alleviate symptoms, individuals can regain control over their lives and improve their quality of life.

Managing symptoms is not just about finding temporary relief; it's about addressing the root causes and finding long-term solutions. When symptoms are left unmanaged, they can lead to a downward spiral of physical and emotional distress. By taking proactive steps to manage symptoms, individuals can break free from this cycle and experience a greater sense of well-being.

Prioritize Sleep: The Foundation of Symptom Management

One of the most important aspects of managing symptoms is prioritizing sleep. Sleep plays a crucial role in our overall health and well-being, and it can have a significant impact on symptom management. When we don't get enough sleep or have poor sleep quality, our symptoms can worsen, making it even more challenging to manage them effectively.

To improve sleep quality, it's essential to establish a consistent sleep routine. This means going to bed and waking up at the same time every day, even on weekends. Creating a relaxing bedtime routine can also help signal to your body that it's time to wind down and prepare for sleep. This could include activities such as reading a book, taking a warm bath, or practicing relaxation techniques like deep breathing or progressive muscle relaxation.

Mindfulness Meditation: A Surprising Solution for Symptom Relief

Mindfulness meditation is a powerful tool for managing symptoms. It involves bringing your attention to the present moment without judgment. By practicing mindfulness meditation regularly, individuals can develop greater awareness of their symptoms and learn to respond to them in a more compassionate and effective way.

To practice mindfulness meditation, find a quiet and comfortable space where you can sit or lie down. Close your eyes and bring your attention to your breath. Notice the sensation of the breath as it enters and leaves your body. If your mind starts to wander, gently bring it back to the breath without judgment. Start with just a few minutes of meditation each day and gradually increase the duration as you become more comfortable.

The Power of Positive Thinking: Changing Your Mindset to Manage Symptoms

Negative thinking can have a significant impact on symptoms. When we constantly focus on our symptoms and view them in a negative light, it can amplify our distress and make it more challenging to manage them effectively. On the other hand, cultivating a positive mindset can help shift our perspective and empower us to take control of our symptoms.

One way to cultivate a positive mindset is by practicing gratitude. Each day, take a few moments to reflect on the things you are grateful for, no matter how small they may seem. This could be anything from a beautiful sunset to a kind gesture from a friend. By focusing on the positive aspects of your life, you can shift your attention away from your symptoms and create a more positive outlook.

Nutrition: The Role of a Healthy Diet in

Symptom Management

Diet plays a crucial role in managing symptoms. Certain foods can exacerbate symptoms, while others can help alleviate them. It's essential to pay attention to how different foods affect your symptoms and make adjustments accordingly.

Incorporating a variety of fruits, vegetables, whole grains, lean proteins, and healthy fats into your diet can provide the nutrients your body needs to function optimally. Avoiding processed foods, sugary snacks, and excessive caffeine can also help reduce inflammation and improve overall well-being.

Exercise: The Benefits of Physical Activity for Symptom Relief

Regular exercise is another powerful tool for managing symptoms. Physical activity releases endorphins, which are natural painkillers and mood boosters. It can also help reduce inflammation, improve sleep quality, and increase overall energy levels.

Finding an exercise routine that works for you is crucial. It's important to choose activities that you enjoy and that are appropriate for your fitness level. This could be anything from walking or swimming to yoga or strength training. Start with small, achievable goals and gradually increase the intensity and duration of your workouts as you build strength and endurance.

Acupuncture: The Surprising Way to Manage Your Symptoms

Acupuncture is an ancient Chinese practice that involves inserting thin needles into specific points on the body. It is believed to help balance the flow of energy, or qi, in the body and promote healing. While the exact mechanisms of how acupuncture works are still not fully understood, many people find it to be an effective way to manage their symptoms.

If you're considering acupuncture, it's important to find a qualified acupuncturist who has received proper training and certification. Ask for recommendations from friends or healthcare professionals, and make sure to inquire about their experience and credentials. During your first visit, the acupuncturist will conduct a thorough assessment and develop a treatment plan tailored to your specific needs.

Music Therapy: A Unique Approach to Symptom Management

Music therapy is a unique approach to managing symptoms that involves using music to address physical, emotional, cognitive, and social needs. It can help reduce pain, anxiety, and depression, improve mood and relaxation, and enhance overall well-being.

Incorporating music therapy into your routine can be as simple as listening to your favorite songs or playing a musical instrument. You can also explore guided imagery exercises that involve visualizing peaceful scenes while listening to calming music. Experiment with different types of music and see what resonates with you the most.

Essential Oils: The Natural Remedy for Symptom Relief

Essential oils are concentrated plant extracts that have been used for centuries for their therapeutic properties. They can be used topically, inhaled, or ingested to help manage symptoms such as pain, stress, anxiety, and insomnia.

When using essential oils, it's important to choose high-quality oils and use them safely. Some oils may cause skin irritation or interact with medications, so it's essential to do your research and consult with a healthcare professional if you have any concerns. You can use essential oils in a diffuser, add a few drops to a carrier oil for massage, or create your own natural remedies.

Massage Therapy: A Surprising Solution for Symptom Management

Massage therapy is another surprising solution for managing symptoms. It involves manipulating the body's soft tissues to promote relaxation, reduce pain and inflammation, and improve overall well-being. Massage can be particularly beneficial for individuals with chronic pain, muscle tension, or stress-related symptoms.

When seeking out a massage therapist, it's important to find someone who is qualified and experienced. Look for therapists who are licensed or certified and have received proper training. During your first visit, communicate your symptoms and goals to the therapist so they can tailor the massage to your specific needs.

Taking Control of Your Symptoms with Surprising Solutions

Managing symptoms is crucial for overall well-being. By prioritizing sleep, practicing mindfulness meditation, cultivating a positive mindset, eating a healthy diet, engaging in regular exercise, exploring alternative therapies like acupuncture and music therapy, using essential oils safely, and incorporating massage therapy into your routine, you can take control of your symptoms and improve your quality of life.

It's important to remember that everyone is different, and what works for one person may not work for another. It may take some trial and error to find the right combination of strategies that work best for you. Be patient with yourself and keep an open mind as you explore different approaches to symptom management. With persistence and a proactive mindset, you can find surprising solutions that help you live a more fulfilling and symptom-free life.

Chapter 12: The Ultimate Guide to 12 Wellness Practices for a Happier Life

In today's fast-paced and stressful world, it is more important than ever to prioritize our well-being. Incorporating wellness practices into our daily lives can have a profound impact on our overall happiness and quality of life. These practices encompass various aspects of our physical, mental, and emotional well-being, and can help us find balance, reduce stress, and cultivate a positive mindset.

By taking the time to care for ourselves and prioritize our well-being, we can experience numerous benefits. These include increased energy levels, improved mental clarity, reduced stress and anxiety, enhanced mood, better sleep quality, and improved physical health. When we make wellness practices a priority, we are better equipped to handle the challenges that life throws at us and can approach each day with a sense of calm and resilience.

The Power of Mindfulness: Techniques for Being Present in the Moment

Mindfulness is the practice of being fully present in the moment, without judgment or attachment to thoughts or emotions. It involves bringing our attention to the present moment and observing our thoughts and sensations without getting caught up in them. By practicing mindfulness, we can cultivate a greater sense of awareness and develop the ability to respond to situations with clarity and compassion.

There are several techniques that can help us cultivate mindfulness in our daily lives. One simple yet powerful technique is deep breathing. By taking slow, deep breaths and focusing on the sensation of the breath entering and leaving our bodies, we can bring ourselves into the present moment and calm our minds. Another technique is body scans, where we systematically bring our attention to different parts of our body, noticing any sensations or tension that may be present. This helps us develop a greater awareness of our bodies and can promote relaxation.

The Benefits of Meditation: How to Start and Maintain a Practice

Meditation is a practice that involves training our minds to focus and redirect our thoughts. It has been practiced for thousands of years and is known for its numerous benefits for mental and emotional well-being. Regular meditation practice can help reduce stress, improve concentration, increase self-awareness, and promote a sense of calm and inner peace.

To start a meditation practice, it is helpful to find a quiet space where you can sit comfortably without distractions. You can start with just a few minutes each day and gradually increase the duration as you become more comfortable. It can be helpful to set a regular schedule for your meditation practice, as this will make it easier to incorporate into your daily routine.

During meditation, you can choose to focus on your breath, a mantra, or simply observe your thoughts without judgment. When your mind wanders, gently bring your attention back to your chosen point of focus. It is important to approach meditation with an open mind and without expectations. It is normal for thoughts to arise during meditation, and the goal is not to stop thinking but rather to observe our thoughts without getting caught up in them.

The Healing Properties of Yoga: Poses and Breathing Exercises for Mind and Body

Yoga is an ancient practice that combines physical postures, breathing exercises, and meditation to promote overall health and well-being. It has been shown to have numerous benefits for both the body and mind.

Regular yoga practice can improve flexibility, strength, balance, and posture. It can also reduce stress, anxiety, and depression, improve sleep quality, and enhance overall mood.

There are many different styles of yoga, ranging from gentle and restorative to more vigorous and challenging. It is important to choose a style that suits your fitness level and interests. Some common yoga poses include downward-facing dog, warrior poses, tree pose, and child's pose. These poses help stretch and strengthen different parts of the body while promoting relaxation and mindfulness.

In addition to physical postures, yoga also incorporates breathing exercises, known as pranayama. These exercises can help calm the mind, reduce stress, and promote relaxation. One simple yet effective breathing exercise is deep belly breathing. To practice this, sit or lie down in a comfortable position and place one hand on your belly. Take slow, deep breaths, allowing your belly to rise and fall with each breath.

The Art of Gratitude: Ways to Cultivate a Positive Attitude and Appreciation

Gratitude is the practice of acknowledging and appreciating the good things in our lives. It involves focusing on the positive aspects of our experiences and expressing gratitude for them. Cultivating gratitude has been shown to have numerous benefits for mental and emotional well-being. It can increase happiness, reduce stress and anxiety, improve relationships, and promote a positive outlook on life.

There are many ways to cultivate gratitude in our daily lives. One simple yet powerful practice is keeping a gratitude journal. Each day, take a few minutes to write down three things you are grateful for. These can be big or small, such as a beautiful sunset, a kind gesture from a friend, or a delicious meal. By regularly reflecting on the things we are grateful for, we can shift our focus from what is lacking in our lives to what we already have.

Another way to cultivate gratitude is through mindfulness. By bringing our attention to the present moment and fully experiencing the sights, sounds, and sensations around us, we can develop a greater appreciation for the simple pleasures in life. Taking the time to savor a cup of tea or enjoy a walk in nature can help us cultivate gratitude and bring more joy into our lives.

The Joy of Journaling: Writing Prompts and Reflections for Self-Discovery

Journaling is a powerful tool for self-discovery and personal growth. It involves writing down our thoughts, feelings, and experiences as a way to gain insight into ourselves and our lives. Journaling can help us process emotions, clarify our thoughts, and gain a deeper understanding of ourselves.

There are many different ways to approach journaling, and it is important to find a style that works for you. Some people prefer to write freely, allowing their thoughts to flow onto the page without judgment or structure. Others find it helpful to use writing prompts or reflection exercises to guide their journaling practice.

Here are a few writing prompts and reflection exercises to get you started:

- Write about a recent challenge or setback you have faced and how you have grown from it.

- Reflect on a time when you felt truly alive and engaged in the present moment. What were you doing? How did it make you feel?

- Write a letter to your younger self, offering words of wisdom and encouragement.

- Make a list of things that bring you joy and make you feel alive. How can you incorporate more of these things into your life?

The Science of Sleep: Tips for Improving Sleep

Quality and Quantity

Sleep is essential for our overall health and well-being. It is during sleep that our bodies repair and regenerate, and our brains process information and consolidate memories. However, many people struggle with sleep issues, such as difficulty falling asleep, staying asleep, or waking up feeling refreshed.

There are several tips that can help improve sleep quality and quantity. One important tip is to establish a consistent bedtime routine. This involves going to bed and waking up at the same time each day, even on weekends. This helps regulate our body's internal clock and can make it easier to fall asleep and wake up naturally.

Another tip is to create a sleep-friendly environment. This includes keeping your bedroom cool, dark, and quiet. You can also try using white noise machines or earplugs to block out any distracting noises. It is also important to avoid screens before bed, as the blue light emitted by electronic devices can interfere with our sleep-wake cycle.

The Value of Exercise: Physical Activities for Health and Happiness

Exercise is not only important for our physical health but also for our mental and emotional well-being. Regular physical activity has been shown to reduce the risk of chronic diseases, improve cardiovascular health, boost mood, reduce stress and anxiety, and enhance overall quality of life.

There are many different types of exercise, and it is important to choose activities that you enjoy and that suit your fitness level. Some examples of physical activities include walking, jogging, swimming, cycling, dancing, yoga, and strength training. Aim for at least 150 minutes of moderate-intensity aerobic activity or 75 minutes of vigorous-intensity aerobic activity each week, along with muscle-strengthening activities on two or more days.

It is also important to listen to your body and give yourself rest days when needed. Overtraining can lead to burnout and increased risk of injury. Remember that exercise should be enjoyable and sustainable, so find activities that you genuinely enjoy and that make you feel good.

The Nourishment of Nutrition: Foods and Habits for a Balanced Diet

A balanced diet is essential for our overall health and well-being. It provides us with the nutrients we need to fuel our bodies, support our immune system, and promote optimal functioning. A healthy diet can also reduce the risk of chronic diseases, such as heart disease, diabetes, and certain types of cancer.

To maintain a balanced diet, it is important to eat a variety of foods from all food groups. This includes fruits, vegetables, whole grains, lean proteins, and healthy fats. Aim to fill half your plate with fruits and vegetables at each meal. Choose whole grains over refined grains whenever possible. Include lean proteins such as poultry, fish, beans, and tofu. And incorporate healthy fats from sources such as avocados, nuts, and olive oil.

In addition to eating a balanced diet, it is important to develop healthy eating habits. This includes eating mindfully, listening to your body's hunger and fullness cues, and practicing portion control. It is also important to stay hydrated by drinking plenty of water throughout the day.

The Connection of Community: Building Relationships and Social Support

Human beings are social creatures, and having strong social connections is essential for our mental health and well-being. Social support can provide us with a sense of belonging, purpose, and connection, and can help us navigate life's challenges with greater ease.

There are many ways to build and maintain relationships. One way is to join a club or organization that aligns with your interests or hobbies. This can provide opportunities to meet like-minded individuals and form new friendships. Another way is to volunteer for a cause that you are passionate about. This not only allows you to give back to your community but also provides opportunities to connect with others who share similar values.

It is also important to nurture existing relationships by making time for the people who are important to you. This can involve scheduling regular catch-ups or outings, sending a thoughtful message or card, or simply reaching out to let someone know you are thinking of them. Building and maintaining relationships takes effort, but the rewards are well worth it.

The Importance of Self-Care: Practices for Taking Care of Yourself Mentally and Emotionally

Self-care is the practice of taking care of ourselves mentally, emotionally, and physically. It involves prioritizing our well-being and making choices that nourish and support us. Self-care looks different for everyone, as it is highly individualized and depends on our unique needs and preferences.

There are many different self-care practices that we can incorporate into our daily lives. Some examples include taking breaks throughout the day to rest and recharge, engaging in activities that bring us joy and relaxation, practicing self-compassion and self-acceptance, setting boundaries and saying no when needed, and seeking support from others when we need it.

It is important to remember that self-care is not selfish or indulgent. It is a necessary practice for maintaining our mental and emotional well-being. By taking care of ourselves, we are better able to show up for others and contribute to the world in a meaningful way.

Conclusion: Recap of the importance of wellness practices for a happier life and encouragement to incorporate them into daily life.

In conclusion, incorporating wellness practices into our daily lives is essential for our overall happiness and well-being. These practices encompass various aspects of our physical, mental, and emotional health and can have a profound impact on our quality of life. By practicing mindfulness, meditation, yoga, gratitude, journaling, prioritizing sleep, engaging in regular exercise, eating a balanced diet, building social connections, and practicing self-care, we can cultivate a greater sense of well-being and live happier, more fulfilling lives. It is important to remember that wellness is a journey, and it takes time and effort to develop these practices. However, the rewards are well worth it. So start small, be consistent, and be kind to yourself along the way. Your well-being is worth it.

Chapter 13: The Science of Emotional Regulation: How to Control Your Feelings

Emotional regulation is the ability to manage and control our emotions in a healthy and constructive way. It plays a crucial role in our overall well-being and can greatly impact our daily lives. When we are able to regulate our emotions effectively, we are better equipped to handle stress, build positive relationships, and navigate through life's challenges. In this article, we will explore the basics of emotional regulation, the role of the brain in emotional control, recognizing emotional triggers, the importance of self-awareness, developing emotional intelligence, strategies for managing anger and frustration, coping with anxiety and stress, techniques for calming the mind and body, cultivating positive emotions and mindset, building resilience through emotional regulation, and seeking professional help for emotional regulation challenges.

Understanding the Basics of Emotional Regulation

Emotional regulation refers to the ability to understand and manage our emotions in a healthy and adaptive way. It involves recognizing and acknowledging our emotions, understanding their underlying causes, and choosing how to respond to them. Emotional regulation is important because it allows us to navigate through life's challenges more effectively. It helps us maintain healthy relationships, make rational decisions, and cope with stress.

Emotional regulation affects our daily lives in various ways. When we are able to regulate our emotions effectively, we are better equipped to handle stressful situations. We are less likely to react impulsively or engage in destructive behaviors. Instead, we can respond in a calm and rational manner. Emotional regulation also plays a role in our relationships. When we are able to regulate our emotions, we can communicate more effectively with others and resolve conflicts in a constructive way.

The Role of the Brain in Emotional Control

The brain plays a crucial role in emotional control. It is responsible for processing and interpreting emotions, as well as regulating their intensity and duration. Different parts of the brain are involved in emotional control, including the amygdala, prefrontal cortex, and hippocampus.

The amygdala is the part of the brain that is responsible for processing emotions, particularly fear and anxiety. It plays a key role in the fight-or-flight response. When we perceive a threat, the amygdala sends signals to other parts of the brain to prepare the body for action. The prefrontal cortex, on the other hand, is responsible for regulating and controlling emotions. It helps us think rationally and make decisions based on logic rather than emotions. The hippocampus is involved in memory formation and retrieval, which is important for emotional regulation as it allows us to learn from past experiences and regulate our emotions accordingly.

Recognizing Your Emotional Triggers

Emotional triggers are events, situations, or people that elicit strong emotional responses. They can vary from person to person, but some common emotional triggers include criticism, rejection, failure, and loss. It is important to recognize your own emotional triggers as they can greatly impact your emotional well-being and how you respond to certain situations.

To identify your own emotional triggers, it can be helpful to pay attention to your emotional reactions in different situations. Notice when you feel a sudden surge of emotion or when you find yourself reacting strongly to something. Reflect on what might have triggered that emotional response and try to identify any patterns or common themes. It can also be helpful to keep a journal where you can record your emotions and any triggers that you notice.

The Importance of Self-Awareness in Emotional Regulation

Self-awareness is the ability to recognize and understand our own thoughts, feelings, and behaviors. It plays a crucial role in emotional regulation because it allows us to identify our emotions, understand their underlying causes, and choose how to respond to them.

Self-awareness helps with emotional regulation by allowing us to recognize when we are experiencing strong emotions and understand why we are feeling that way. This awareness gives us the opportunity to pause and reflect before reacting impulsively. It also allows us to identify any patterns or triggers that may be contributing to our emotional responses. By being self-aware, we can take steps to manage our emotions in a healthy and constructive way.

There are various techniques that can help improve self-awareness. Mindfulness meditation, for example, is a practice that involves paying attention to the present moment without judgment. It can help us become more aware of our thoughts, feelings, and bodily sensations. Journaling is another effective technique for improving self-awareness. By writing down our thoughts and emotions, we can gain insight into our own patterns and triggers.

Developing Emotional Intelligence

Emotional intelligence refers to the ability to recognize, understand, and manage our own emotions, as well as the emotions of others. It plays a crucial role in emotional regulation because it allows us to navigate through social interactions more effectively and build positive relationships.

Developing emotional intelligence involves several key skills. Firstly, it involves self-awareness, as mentioned earlier. Secondly, it involves self-regulation, which is the ability to control and manage our own emotions. This includes being able to calm ourselves down when we are feeling overwhelmed or angry. Thirdly, it involves empathy, which is the ability to understand and share the feelings of others. This allows us to connect with others on a deeper level and respond to their emotions in a supportive way. Lastly, it involves effective communication, which is the ability to express our emotions and needs in a clear and respectful manner.

There are various ways to develop emotional intelligence. One way is through self-reflection and introspection. Taking the time to reflect on our own emotions and behaviors can help us gain insight into ourselves and others. Another way is through practicing empathy and active listening. By putting ourselves in someone else's shoes and truly listening to their perspective, we can develop a better understanding of their emotions and needs.

Strategies for Managing Anger and Frustration

Anger and frustration are common emotions that can be difficult to manage. They can arise from various triggers, such as feeling misunderstood, being treated unfairly, or experiencing a loss of control. However, it is important to manage these emotions in a healthy and constructive way to avoid damaging relationships and causing harm to ourselves.

One technique for managing anger and frustration is deep breathing. When we are angry or frustrated, our breathing tends to become shallow and rapid. By taking slow, deep breaths, we can activate the body's relaxation response and calm ourselves down. Another technique is to practice mindfulness. This involves bringing our attention to the present moment and accepting our emotions without judgment. By observing our anger or frustration without reacting to it, we can gain a sense of control over our emotions.

Preventing anger and frustration from escalating is also important. One way to do this is by taking a time-out. If you feel yourself becoming overwhelmed with anger or frustration, take a break from the situation and give yourself some time to cool down. Engaging in physical activity can also help release pent-up energy and reduce feelings of anger or frustration.

Coping with Anxiety and Stress

Anxiety and stress are common emotions that can have a significant impact on our well-being if not managed effectively. They can arise from various triggers, such as work pressure, financial difficulties, or relationship problems. However, there are techniques that can help us cope with anxiety and stress in a healthy way.

One technique for coping with anxiety and stress is progressive muscle relaxation. This involves tensing and then relaxing different muscle groups in the body, which can help promote relaxation and reduce feelings of tension. Another technique is cognitive restructuring, which involves challenging negative thoughts and replacing them with more positive and realistic ones. By changing our thought patterns, we can reduce anxiety and stress.

Engaging in activities that promote relaxation and self-care is also important for coping with anxiety and stress. This can include activities such as taking a bath, practicing yoga or meditation, or engaging in hobbies that bring joy and relaxation. It is also important to prioritize self-care by getting enough sleep, eating a balanced diet, and engaging in regular physical activity.

Techniques for Calming the Mind and Body

There are various techniques that can help calm the mind and body, promoting relaxation and reducing stress. These techniques can be incorporated into your daily routine to help manage emotions more effectively.

One technique is deep breathing. By taking slow, deep breaths, you can activate the body's relaxation response and calm yourself down. Another technique is progressive muscle relaxation, which involves tensing and then relaxing different muscle groups in the body. This can help promote relaxation and reduce feelings of tension.

Practicing mindfulness is another effective technique for calming the mind and body. This involves bringing your attention to the present moment and accepting your thoughts and emotions without judgment. By observing your thoughts and emotions without reacting to them, you can gain a sense of control over your mind.

Engaging in activities that promote relaxation, such as taking a bath, practicing yoga or meditation, or listening to calming music, can also help calm the mind and body. It is important to find activities that work best for you and incorporate them into your daily routine.

Cultivating Positive Emotions and Mindset

Cultivating positive emotions and mindset is important for overall well-being and emotional regulation. Positive emotions, such as joy, gratitude, and love, can help counteract negative emotions and promote resilience.

One technique for cultivating positive emotions is practicing gratitude. This involves taking the time to reflect on the things you are grateful for in your life. By focusing on the positive aspects of your life, you can shift your mindset towards a more positive outlook.

Engaging in activities that bring joy and happiness is also important for cultivating positive emotions. This can include activities such as spending time with loved ones, pursuing hobbies that bring joy, or engaging in acts of kindness towards others.

It is also important to challenge negative thought patterns and replace them with more positive and realistic ones. By reframing negative thoughts, you can shift your mindset towards a more positive outlook.

Building Resilience through Emotional Regulation

Resilience refers to the ability to bounce back from adversity and navigate through life's challenges. Emotional regulation plays a crucial role in building resilience because it allows us to manage and cope with difficult emotions in a healthy and constructive way.

One way emotional regulation helps build resilience is by allowing us to recognize and acknowledge our emotions. By understanding our emotions, we can better navigate through difficult situations and make rational decisions. Emotional regulation also helps us develop effective coping strategies for managing stress and adversity. By learning how to regulate our emotions, we can respond to challenges in a calm and rational manner.

Practicing self-care is also important for building resilience. This can include engaging in activities that promote relaxation and well-being, such as practicing mindfulness, engaging in regular physical activity, or spending time with loved ones.

Seeking Professional Help for Emotional Regulation Challenges

While practicing emotional regulation techniques can be helpful, there may be times when professional help is needed. If you are struggling with emotional regulation challenges that are significantly impacting your daily life, relationships, or overall well-being, it may be beneficial to seek the help of a mental health professional.

There are different types of professionals who can help with emotional regulation challenges, including therapists, counselors, psychologists, and psychiatrists. It is important to find the right professional for your needs. Consider factors such as their area of expertise, their approach to therapy, and their availability.

You can find a mental health professional by asking for recommendations from your primary care physician, reaching out to your insurance provider for a list of in-network providers, or searching online directories. It is important to remember that seeking professional help is a sign of strength and self-care.

Emotional regulation is a crucial skill that plays a significant role in our overall well-being and daily lives. By understanding the basics of emotional regulation, recognizing our emotional triggers, developing self-awareness and emotional intelligence, and practicing strategies for managing anger, frustration, anxiety, and stress, we can navigate through life's challenges more effectively. Cultivating positive emotions and mindset, building resilience, and seeking professional help when needed are also important aspects of emotional regulation. By practicing these techniques regularly, we can improve our emotional well-being and lead healthier and more fulfilling lives.

Chapter 14: From Shy to Confident: Strategies for Building Strong Social Connections

Social connections play a crucial role in our lives, impacting our mental health, well-being, and overall happiness. Whether it's with family, friends, or even acquaintances, these connections provide us with a sense of belonging and support. In this article, we will explore the importance of social connections and discuss various strategies for overcoming shyness, building self-confidence, developing active listening skills, starting conversations, finding common ground, navigating social situations, building lasting relationships, embracing diversity, and building a support network.

Understanding the Importance of Social Connections

Social connections are vital for our mental health and well-being. They provide us with emotional support, a sense of belonging, and a feeling of being understood and valued. When we have strong social connections, we are more likely to experience lower levels of stress, anxiety, and depression. On the other hand, social isolation can have negative effects on our mental health.

Research has shown that individuals who lack social connections are at a higher risk of developing mental health issues such as depression and anxiety. Social isolation can also lead to feelings of loneliness and low self-esteem. Therefore, it is crucial to prioritize building and maintaining social connections in our lives.

Overcoming Shyness: Tips and Techniques

Shyness can often hinder our ability to form social connections. However, there are strategies that can help us overcome shyness and step out of our comfort zone. One effective technique is practicing social skills. By actively engaging in social situations and practicing conversation starters or small talk, we can gradually become more comfortable in social settings.

Another technique is exposure therapy. This involves gradually exposing ourselves to situations that make us feel shy or uncomfortable. By gradually increasing our exposure to these situations, we can desensitize ourselves to the anxiety they may cause.

Stepping out of our comfort zone is essential for personal growth and building social connections. By challenging ourselves to try new things and meet new people, we can expand our social circle and develop stronger connections.

Building Self-Confidence: A Key to Strong Social Connections

Self-confidence plays a crucial role in our ability to form and maintain social connections. When we feel confident in ourselves and our abilities, we are more likely to engage in social interactions and express ourselves authentically.

One way to build self-confidence is through positive self-talk. By replacing negative thoughts with positive affirmations, we can boost our self-esteem and develop a more positive self-image. Setting achievable goals is another effective strategy for building self-confidence. By setting small, attainable goals and celebrating our successes, we can gradually build our confidence over time.

When we have self-confidence, we are more likely to engage in social interactions without fear of judgment or rejection. This can lead to more meaningful connections and a greater sense of belonging.

The Power of Positive Thinking in Social Settings

Positive thinking can have a significant impact on our social interactions. When we approach social situations with a positive mindset, we are more likely to engage in conversations, express ourselves authentically, and connect with others on a deeper level.

Cultivating a positive mindset involves focusing on the present moment and reframing negative thoughts into positive ones. For example, instead of thinking, "I'm not good at making conversation," we can reframe it as, "I have interesting things to share, and people will enjoy talking to me."

By adopting a positive mindset, we can overcome self-doubt and insecurities, allowing us to form stronger social connections.

Developing Active Listening Skills for Better Communication

Active listening is a crucial skill for effective communication and building strong social connections. When we actively listen to others, we show them that we value their thoughts and opinions, which can lead to deeper connections and more meaningful conversations.

To improve active listening skills, it is important to focus on the speaker and avoid distractions. This means putting away our phones, maintaining eye contact, and giving our full attention to the person speaking. It is also helpful to ask clarifying questions and paraphrase what the speaker has said to ensure understanding.

By developing active listening skills, we can enhance our communication abilities and foster stronger connections with others.

Breaking the Ice: Effective Ways to Start Conversations

Starting conversations can be intimidating, especially with strangers or acquaintances. However, initiating conversations is essential for building social connections and expanding our social circle.

One effective way to break the ice is by asking open-ended questions. These questions encourage the other person to share more about themselves and can lead to more engaging conversations. For example, instead of asking a closed-ended question like, "Do you like sports?" we can ask an open-ended question like, "What sports do you enjoy playing or watching?"

Another effective technique is finding common ground. By identifying shared interests or experiences, we can create a connection and build rapport with the other person. For example, if we discover that we both enjoy hiking, we can discuss our favorite trails or share hiking tips.

By initiating conversations and finding common ground, we can form new connections and expand our social network.

Finding Common Ground: How to Connect with Others

Finding common ground is essential for connecting with others on a deeper level. When we share similar interests or values with someone, it creates a sense of connection and understanding.

One strategy for finding common ground is actively seeking out shared interests. This can involve joining clubs or organizations related to our hobbies or passions. By engaging in activities that align with our interests, we are more likely to meet like-minded individuals and form stronger connections.

Another strategy is exploring shared values. By discussing topics such as personal values, beliefs, or goals, we can identify commonalities with others and develop a deeper understanding of each other.

By finding common ground, we can create a foundation for meaningful connections and foster a sense of belonging.

Navigating Social Situations: Coping with Anxiety and Nervousness

Social anxiety and nervousness can often hinder our ability to form social connections. However, there are strategies that can help us cope with these feelings and navigate social situations more effectively.

One tip is to practice deep breathing exercises. Deep breathing can help calm our nervous system and reduce anxiety. By taking slow, deep breaths and focusing on our breath, we can alleviate feelings of nervousness and approach social situations with a calmer mindset.

Another strategy is to face our fears gradually. By gradually exposing ourselves to situations that make us anxious, we can desensitize ourselves to the fear and build confidence over time. This can involve starting with small social interactions and gradually working our way up to more challenging situations.

Seeking support from trusted friends or family members can also be beneficial. By sharing our feelings of anxiety or nervousness with someone we trust, we can gain perspective and receive encouragement.

By coping with anxiety and nervousness, we can overcome barriers to forming social connections and engage more fully in social interactions.

Building Lasting Relationships: Strategies for Maintaining Connections

Building lasting relationships requires effort and commitment. It is important to invest time and energy into maintaining connections with others to ensure the longevity of the relationship.

One tip for maintaining relationships is regular communication. This can involve scheduling regular catch-ups or phone calls with friends or family members. By staying in touch consistently, we can strengthen our connections and show others that they are valued.

Another strategy is showing appreciation. By expressing gratitude for the people in our lives and acknowledging their contributions, we can foster a sense of mutual respect and deepen our connections.

It is also important to be supportive of others during challenging times. By offering a listening ear, providing encouragement, or helping in practical ways, we can demonstrate our commitment to the relationship and strengthen the bond.

By implementing these strategies, we can build and maintain lasting relationships that bring joy and fulfillment to our lives.

Embracing Diversity: Celebrating Differences in Social Settings

Embracing diversity is essential for creating inclusive and welcoming social environments. When we celebrate differences and appreciate the unique perspectives of others, we foster a sense of belonging and create opportunities for growth and learning.

One way to embrace diversity is by actively seeking out diverse perspectives. This can involve engaging in conversations with individuals from different backgrounds or cultures and listening to their experiences and viewpoints. By actively seeking out diverse perspectives, we can broaden our own understanding of the world and develop empathy for others.

Another strategy is challenging our own biases and assumptions. By examining our own beliefs and questioning stereotypes, we can become more open-minded and accepting of others.

By embracing diversity, we create a more inclusive society where everyone feels valued and respected.

Building a Support Network: The Importance of Having Strong Social Connections

Having a support network is crucial for our mental health and well-being. A support network consists of individuals who provide emotional support, guidance, and encouragement during challenging times.

One tip for building a support network is to reach out to friends or family members who are supportive and understanding. By nurturing these relationships, we can create a strong foundation of support in our lives.

Another strategy is to join support groups or communities related to our interests or challenges. These groups provide a space for individuals with similar experiences to connect, share advice, and offer support.

It is also important to be proactive in seeking support when needed. By reaching out to trusted individuals when we are struggling, we can receive the help and guidance necessary to navigate difficult situations.

By building a support network, we create a safety net that provides us with the emotional support and encouragement needed to thrive.

In conclusion, social connections are essential for our mental health, well-being, and overall happiness. By implementing the tips and strategies discussed in this article, we can overcome shyness, build self-confidence, develop active listening skills, start conversations, find common ground, navigate social situations, build lasting relationships, embrace diversity, and build a support network. By prioritizing social connections in our lives, we can experience a greater sense of belonging, support, and fulfillment.

Chapter 15: Stress Management 101: How to Stay Calm and Focused in a Busy World

Stress is an inevitable part of life, and managing it effectively is crucial for our overall health and well-being. In today's fast-paced world, stress has become a common occurrence, and if left unchecked, it can have detrimental effects on our physical and mental health. Therefore, it is essential to understand the basics of stress management and develop strategies to cope with it effectively.

Understanding the Basics of Stress Management

Stress can be defined as the body's response to any demand or threat. When we encounter a stressful situation, our body releases stress hormones such as cortisol and adrenaline, which trigger the "fight or flight" response. While this response is necessary in certain situations, chronic stress can lead to a range of health problems, including high blood pressure, heart disease, depression, and anxiety.

Managing stress is crucial for maintaining our overall health and well-being. By implementing effective stress management techniques, we can reduce the negative impact of stress on our bodies and minds. Stress management involves identifying the causes of stress in our lives and developing strategies to cope with them effectively.

Common Causes of Stress and How to Identify Them

Stress can be caused by various factors, including work-related pressures, relationship issues, financial difficulties, and health problems. It is important to identify the specific stressors in our lives in order to effectively manage them.

Work-related stress is a common cause of stress for many individuals. Long hours, tight deadlines, and demanding bosses can all contribute to feelings of overwhelm and anxiety. Relationship issues, whether with a partner, family member, or friend, can also be a significant source of stress. Financial difficulties can cause a great deal of worry and anxiety as well.

To identify personal stress triggers, it is important to pay attention to our thoughts, emotions, and physical sensations when we feel stressed. Keeping a journal can be helpful in identifying patterns and triggers. Additionally, seeking support from a therapist or counselor can provide valuable insights into the causes of stress in our lives.

The Importance of Self-Care in Managing Stress

Self-care plays a crucial role in managing stress effectively. It involves taking deliberate actions to prioritize our physical, mental, and emotional well-being. Engaging in self-care activities can help reduce stress levels and improve our overall quality of life.

Self-care activities can vary from person to person, but some common examples include exercise, meditation, engaging in hobbies, spending time in nature, and practicing relaxation techniques. Engaging in regular exercise has been shown to reduce stress levels by releasing endorphins, which are natural mood boosters. Meditation and mindfulness practices can help calm the mind and reduce anxiety. Engaging in hobbies and activities that bring joy and fulfillment can also provide a much-needed break from the stresses of daily life.

Simple Techniques for Relaxation and Stress Relief

There are several simple techniques that can be used for relaxation and stress relief. These techniques can be easily incorporated into our daily routines and can help us manage stress more effectively.

One effective technique is deep breathing exercises. Deep breathing helps activate the body's relaxation response and reduces the production of stress hormones. To practice deep breathing, find a quiet space, sit or lie down comfortably, and take slow, deep breaths in through the nose and out through the mouth.

Progressive muscle relaxation is another technique that can help reduce stress levels. This technique involves tensing and then relaxing each muscle group in the body, starting from the toes and working up to the head. By consciously relaxing each muscle group, we can release tension and promote relaxation.

Visualization techniques can also be helpful in reducing stress. By imagining ourselves in a calm and peaceful environment, we can create a sense of relaxation and tranquility. Visualization can be done by closing our eyes and imagining ourselves in a place that brings us joy and peace.

Developing a Positive Mindset for Stress Reduction

Developing a positive mindset is crucial for effective stress management. Our thoughts and beliefs play a significant role in how we perceive and respond to stress. By cultivating a positive mindset, we can reduce the impact of stress on our lives.

Positive thinking involves focusing on the positive aspects of a situation and reframing negative thoughts into more positive ones. This can be done by practicing gratitude, challenging negative thoughts, and surrounding ourselves with positive influences. By shifting our mindset from one of negativity and worry to one of positivity and optimism, we can reduce stress levels and improve our overall well-being.

The Role of Exercise in Stress Management

Exercise is a powerful tool for managing stress. Physical activity has been shown to reduce stress levels by increasing the production of endorphins, which are natural mood boosters. Regular exercise can also improve sleep quality, boost self-confidence, and provide a healthy outlet for stress and tension.

There are various types of exercises that can be effective in reducing stress levels. Aerobic exercises such as running, swimming, or cycling can help release tension and promote relaxation. Yoga and Pilates are also excellent options for reducing stress, as they combine physical movement with mindfulness and deep breathing.

It is important to find an exercise routine that suits our individual preferences and needs. By incorporating regular exercise into our daily routines, we can effectively manage stress and improve our overall well-being.

Tips for Managing Work-Related Stress

Work-related stress is a common cause of stress for many individuals. Managing work-related stress is crucial for maintaining our mental health and well-being. Here are some strategies that can help:

1. Prioritize tasks: Make a to-do list and prioritize tasks based on their importance and urgency. This will help you stay organized and focused.

2. Set boundaries: Establish clear boundaries between work and personal life. Avoid checking emails or working during non-work hours.

3. Take breaks: Take regular breaks throughout the day to rest and recharge. Use this time to engage in activities that help you relax and reduce stress.

4. Seek support: Reach out to colleagues, friends, or family members for support and guidance. Talking about your stressors can help alleviate some of the pressure.

5. Practice time management: Learn effective time management techniques to help you stay on top of your workload and avoid feeling overwhelmed.

Strategies for Dealing with Family and Relationship Stress

Family and relationship stress can be a significant source of stress in our lives. Here are some strategies for managing family and relationship stress:

1. Improve communication: Effective communication is key to resolving conflicts and reducing stress in relationships. Practice active listening and express your thoughts and feelings openly and honestly.

2. Set boundaries: Establish clear boundaries with family members or loved ones to protect your own well-being. Learn to say no when necessary and prioritize your own needs.

3. Seek support: Reach out to a therapist or counselor for guidance and support in navigating relationship issues. They can provide valuable insights and strategies for managing stress in relationships.

4. Practice forgiveness: Holding onto grudges and resentment can contribute to ongoing stress in relationships. Practice forgiveness and let go of past hurts to promote healing and reduce stress.

5. Take time for yourself: Prioritize self-care activities that bring you joy and fulfillment. Taking time for yourself can help reduce stress levels and improve your overall well-being.

The Benefits of Mindfulness and Meditation

Mindfulness and meditation are powerful tools for managing stress and promoting overall well-being. Mindfulness involves paying attention to the present moment without judgment, while meditation involves focusing the mind on a specific object or activity.

Incorporating mindfulness and meditation into a stress management routine can have numerous benefits. These practices can help reduce anxiety, improve focus and concentration, promote relaxation, and increase self-awareness. By practicing mindfulness and meditation regularly, we can develop a greater sense of calm and resilience in the face of stress.

How to Create a Stress-Free Environment at Home and Work

Creating a stress-free environment is crucial for managing stress effectively. Here are some tips for creating a calming environment:

1. Declutter: Remove unnecessary clutter from your physical space. A clutter-free environment can promote a sense of calm and reduce feelings of overwhelm.

2. Create a peaceful atmosphere: Use calming colors, soft lighting, and soothing scents to create a peaceful atmosphere in your home or workspace. Consider incorporating elements of nature, such as plants or natural materials, to promote relaxation.

3. Minimize distractions: Identify and minimize distractions that contribute to stress, such as excessive noise or visual clutter. Create a designated space for work or relaxation that is free from distractions.

4. Establish routines: Establishing daily routines can provide structure and reduce stress levels. Create a schedule that includes time for self-care, relaxation, and activities that bring you joy.

5. Practice self-compassion: Be kind and compassionate towards yourself. Treat yourself with the same care and understanding that you would offer to a loved one.

Seeking Professional Help for Chronic Stress and

Anxiety

While self-help strategies can be effective in managing stress, there may be times when professional help is necessary. If chronic stress or anxiety is significantly impacting your daily life and well-being, it may be beneficial to seek support from a mental health professional.

Therapists, counselors, and psychologists are trained to help individuals manage stress and anxiety effectively. They can provide valuable insights, strategies, and support in navigating the challenges of stress management. Additionally, they can help identify any underlying issues that may be contributing to chronic stress or anxiety.

In conclusion, managing stress is crucial for our overall health and well-being. By understanding the basics of stress management and implementing effective strategies, we can reduce the negative impact of stress on our bodies and minds. It is important to identify the causes of stress in our lives, practice self-care, and develop a positive mindset. Additionally, incorporating relaxation techniques, exercise, and mindfulness practices can help reduce stress levels. By creating a stress-free environment and seeking professional help when necessary, we can prioritize stress management and improve our overall quality of life.

16: The Ultimate Guide to Setting Achievable Goals in 2021

Setting goals is an essential aspect of personal growth and success. It provides individuals with direction, motivation, and a sense of purpose. As we enter 2021, it is more important than ever to set goals that will help us navigate the challenges and uncertainties of the year ahead. In this article, we will explore why setting goals is crucial for personal growth and success in 2021, how to identify priorities and values to set meaningful goals, the SMART method for setting effective goals, the power of visualization, strategies for overcoming obstacles and staying motivated, the role of accountability in goal setting, the importance of celebrating small wins, the need for flexibility in goal setting, avoiding burnout, tracking progress, and creating a personalized action plan for achieving goals in 2021.

Why Setting Goals is Important for Personal Growth and Success in 2021

Setting goals provides numerous benefits that contribute to personal growth and success. Firstly, it increases motivation. When we have clear goals in mind, we are more likely to feel motivated to take action and work towards achieving them. Goals give us something to strive for and provide a sense of purpose.

Secondly, setting goals helps us stay focused. With so many distractions and demands on our time, it can be easy to lose sight of what truly matters. By setting goals, we can prioritize our efforts and concentrate on what is most important to us.

Thirdly, setting goals enhances productivity. When we have a clear vision of what we want to achieve, we can create a plan of action and allocate our time and resources effectively. This leads to increased productivity and efficiency.

Moreover, setting goals contributes to overall well-being. When we have a sense of purpose and are actively working towards something meaningful, it boosts our self-esteem and satisfaction with life. It gives us a sense of accomplishment and fulfillment.

How to Identify Your Priorities and Values to Set Meaningful Goals

Before setting goals, it is crucial to identify our priorities and values. This step ensures that our goals align with what truly matters to us and increases the likelihood of achieving them.

One way to identify priorities and values is through journaling. Take some time to reflect on what brings you joy, fulfillment, and a sense of purpose. Write down your thoughts and feelings, and pay attention to recurring themes or patterns. This will help you gain clarity on what is most important to you.

Another strategy is self-reflection exercises. Engage in activities such as meditation, mindfulness, or deep introspection. These practices can help you connect with your inner self and uncover your core values and priorities.

It is also helpful to seek feedback from trusted friends or mentors. Sometimes, others can provide valuable insights and perspectives that we may not have considered ourselves.

The SMART Method: A Step-by-Step Guide to Setting Specific, Measurable, Achievable, Relevant, and Time-bound Goals

The SMART method is a popular framework for setting effective goals. It stands for Specific, Measurable, Achievable, Relevant, and Time-bound.

Specific goals are clear and well-defined. Instead of saying "I want to exercise more," a specific goal would be "I want to exercise for 30 minutes, three times a week."

Measurable goals have quantifiable criteria for success. For example, instead of saying "I want to save money," a measurable goal would be "I want to save $500 per month."

Achievable goals are realistic and within reach. It is important to set goals that challenge us but are still attainable. Setting unrealistic goals can lead to frustration and discouragement.

Relevant goals are aligned with our priorities and values. They should be meaningful and contribute to our overall well-being.

Time-bound goals have a specific deadline or timeframe attached to them. This helps create a sense of urgency and accountability. Instead of saying "I want to learn a new language," a time-bound goal would be "I want to learn conversational Spanish within six months."

By applying the SMART method to our goals, we increase the likelihood of success and ensure that our goals are well-defined and aligned with our priorities and values.

The Power of Visualization: How to Visualize Your Goals and Make Them a Reality

Visualization is a powerful technique that can help us achieve our goals. It involves creating vivid mental images of what we want to accomplish and experiencing the emotions associated with achieving those goals.

One way to visualize goals is by creating a vision board. A vision board is a collage of images, words, and quotes that represent our goals and aspirations. By looking at our vision board regularly, we reinforce our intentions and keep our goals at the forefront of our minds.

Another strategy is guided meditation. There are numerous guided meditations available that specifically focus on visualizing goals. These meditations guide us through the process of imagining ourselves achieving our goals and experiencing the emotions associated with that success.

Visualization helps us tap into the power of our subconscious mind. When we consistently visualize our goals, we program our minds to seek out opportunities and take actions that align with those goals.

It increases our belief in ourselves and our ability to achieve what we desire.

Overcoming Obstacles and Staying Motivated: Tips and Strategies for Achieving Your Goals

While setting goals is important, it is equally crucial to anticipate and overcome obstacles that may arise along the way. Here are some tips and strategies for staying motivated and overcoming obstacles:

1. Break goals down into smaller tasks: Sometimes, big goals can feel overwhelming. By breaking them down into smaller, more manageable tasks, we can make progress and stay motivated.

2. Seek support from others: Surround yourself with people who support your goals and can provide encouragement and guidance when needed. Joining a mastermind group or finding an accountability partner can be beneficial.

3. Stay flexible: It is important to be adaptable and open to change. Circumstances may shift, and it is essential to adjust our goals and plans accordingly.

4. Practice self-care: Taking care of ourselves physically, mentally, and emotionally is crucial for staying motivated. Make sure to prioritize self-care activities such as exercise, rest, and relaxation.

5. Celebrate progress: Celebrating small wins along the way can boost motivation and provide a sense of accomplishment. Take time to acknowledge and reward yourself for the progress you have made.

The Role of Accountability in Goal Setting: How to Stay Accountable to Yourself and Others

Accountability plays a significant role in goal setting. When we hold ourselves accountable, we are more likely to stay committed and take consistent action towards our goals. Here are some tips for staying accountable:

1. Set deadlines: Assign specific deadlines to your goals and tasks. This creates a sense of urgency and helps you stay on track.

2. Share your goals with others: By sharing your goals with a trusted friend or mentor, you create a sense of external accountability. They can provide support, encouragement, and hold you accountable to your commitments.

3. Track your progress: Regularly monitor your progress towards your goals. This can be done through journaling, using a planner or tracking app, or setting regular check-ins with yourself or others.

4. Reflect on setbacks: If you encounter setbacks or obstacles, take the time to reflect on what went wrong and how you can learn from the experience. Use setbacks as opportunities for growth and improvement.

5. Be honest with yourself: It is important to be honest with yourself about your progress and efforts towards your goals. If you find yourself slacking or losing motivation, take the time to reassess and recommit to your goals.

Celebrating Small Wins: Why Celebrating Milestones Can Help You Stay Focused and Motivated

Celebrating small wins is an essential aspect of goal setting. It provides a sense of accomplishment, boosts motivation, and helps us stay focused on our long-term goals. Here are some tips for celebrating milestones:

1. Reward yourself: When you achieve a milestone or make significant progress towards your goals, reward yourself with something meaningful. It could be a small treat, a day off, or a special activity that brings you joy.

2. Reflect on accomplishments: Take the time to reflect on what you have achieved and how far you have come. Write down your accomplishments and express gratitude for your efforts.

3. Share your success: Share your achievements with others who have supported you along the way. Celebrate with friends, family, or colleagues who have been part of your journey.

4. Take a break: Sometimes, it is important to take a break and recharge. Celebrating milestones can involve taking time off to rest and rejuvenate before moving on to the next phase of your goals.

Celebrating small wins not only boosts motivation but also reinforces positive habits and behaviors that contribute to long-term success.

The Importance of Flexibility in Goal Setting: How to Adjust Your Goals as Circumstances Change

Flexibility is crucial in goal setting, especially in times of uncertainty and change. It is important to be adaptable and willing to adjust our goals as circumstances evolve. Here are some tips for maintaining flexibility:

1. Reevaluate priorities: Regularly reassess your priorities and values to ensure that your goals align with what is most important to you at any given time.

2. Set new deadlines: If circumstances change or unexpected events occur, be willing to adjust your deadlines or timelines accordingly. This allows for more realistic goal setting and reduces the likelihood of feeling overwhelmed or discouraged.

3. Seek feedback: Be open to feedback from trusted friends, mentors, or coaches. They can provide valuable insights and perspectives that may help you adjust your goals or approach.

4. Embrace change: Instead of resisting change, embrace it as an opportunity for growth and learning. Be willing to let go of goals that no longer serve you and embrace new opportunities that align with your evolving priorities.

Flexibility in goal setting allows us to adapt to changing circumstances and ensures that our goals remain relevant and meaningful.

Avoiding Burnout: How to Set Realistic Goals and Manage Your Time Effectively

Avoiding burnout is crucial for long-term success and well-being. Setting realistic goals and managing time effectively are essential strategies for preventing burnout. Here are some tips:

1. Set realistic goals: Be honest with yourself about what you can realistically achieve within a given timeframe. Setting overly ambitious goals can lead to burnout and disappointment.

2. Prioritize tasks: Identify the most important tasks that will contribute to your goals and focus on those first. This helps prevent overwhelm and ensures that you are allocating your time and energy effectively.

3. Delegate or outsource: If possible, delegate tasks or outsource certain responsibilities to free up your time and energy for more important activities.

4. Take breaks: Regularly schedule breaks throughout your day to rest, recharge, and prevent burnout. This could involve short breaks during work hours or longer breaks such as vacations or weekends off.

5. Practice self-care: Prioritize self-care activities such as exercise, rest, relaxation, and hobbies. Taking care of yourself physically, mentally, and emotionally is crucial for preventing burnout.

By setting realistic goals and managing your time effectively, you can maintain a healthy work-life balance and avoid burnout.

The Benefits of Tracking Your Progress: How to Monitor Your Success and Stay on Track

Tracking progress is an essential aspect of goal setting. It allows us to monitor our success, stay on track, and make adjustments as needed. Here are some tips for tracking progress:

1. Use a planner or journal: Write down your goals, tasks, and progress in a planner or journal. This provides a visual representation of your progress and helps you stay organized.

2. Set regular check-ins: Schedule regular check-ins with yourself to assess your progress towards your goals. This could be weekly, monthly, or quarterly, depending on the nature of your goals.

3. Celebrate milestones: As mentioned earlier, celebrating milestones is an important part of tracking progress. It provides motivation and reinforces positive habits and behaviors.

4. Seek feedback: Ask for feedback from trusted friends, mentors, or coaches. They can provide insights and perspectives that may help you adjust your goals or approach.

5. Adjust as needed: If you find that you are not making progress or encountering obstacles, be willing to adjust your goals or strategies. Flexibility is key in goal setting.

Tracking progress allows us to stay accountable, make adjustments when necessary, and maintain momentum towards our goals.

Putting It All Together: Creating a Personalized Action Plan for Achieving Your Goals in 2021

Now that we have explored various strategies for goal setting and achievement, it is time to put it all together and create a personalized action plan for achieving your goals in 2021. Here is a step-by-step guide:

1. Identify your priorities and values: Reflect on what is most important to you and what you want to achieve in the year ahead.

2. Set SMART goals: Use the SMART method to set specific, measurable, achievable, relevant, and time-bound goals that align with your priorities and values.

3. Visualize your goals: Create a vision board or engage in guided meditations to visualize your goals and reinforce your intentions.

4. Overcome obstacles and stay motivated: Develop strategies for overcoming obstacles and staying motivated, such as breaking goals down into smaller tasks and seeking support from others.

5. Stay accountable: Set deadlines, share your goals with others, track your progress, and reflect on setbacks to stay accountable to yourself and others.

6. Celebrate milestones: Celebrate small wins along the way to boost motivation and acknowledge your progress.

7. Be flexible: Be willing to adjust your goals and plans as circumstances change. Regularly reassess your priorities and values to ensure that your goals remain relevant and meaningful.

8. Avoid burnout: Set realistic goals, manage your time effectively, and prioritize self-care to prevent burnout.

9. Track your progress: Use a planner or journal, set regular check-ins, seek feedback, and make adjustments as needed to stay on track towards your goals.

10. Take action: Finally, take action and start working towards your goals. Break them down into actionable steps and commit to consistent effort and progress.

Setting goals is crucial for personal growth and success in 2021. It provides direction, motivation, and a sense of purpose. By identifying priorities and values, using the SMART method, visualizing goals, overcoming obstacles, staying accountable, celebrating milestones, embracing flexibility, avoiding burnout, tracking progress, and creating a personalized action plan, individuals can set meaningful goals and work towards achieving them in the year ahead. It is time to take action and make 2021 a year of growth and success.

16: The Ultimate Guide to Setting Achievable Goals in 2021

Setting goals is an essential aspect of personal growth and success. It provides individuals with direction, motivation, and a sense of purpose. As we enter 2021, it is more important than ever to set goals that will help us navigate the challenges and uncertainties of the year ahead. In this article, we will explore why setting goals is crucial for personal growth and success in 2021, how to identify priorities and values to set meaningful goals, the SMART method for setting effective goals, the power of visualization, strategies for overcoming obstacles and staying motivated, the role of accountability in goal setting, the importance of celebrating small wins, the need for flexibility in goal setting, avoiding burnout, tracking progress, and creating a personalized action plan for achieving goals in 2021.

Why Setting Goals is Important for Personal Growth and Success in 2021

Setting goals provides numerous benefits that contribute to personal growth and success. Firstly, it increases motivation. When we have clear goals in mind, we are more likely to feel motivated to take action and work towards achieving them. Goals give us something to strive for and provide a sense of purpose.

Secondly, setting goals helps us stay focused. With so many distractions and demands on our time, it can be easy to lose sight of what truly matters. By setting goals, we can prioritize our efforts and concentrate on what is most important to us.

Thirdly, setting goals enhances productivity. When we have a clear vision of what we want to achieve, we can create a plan of action and allocate our time and resources effectively. This leads to increased productivity and efficiency.

Moreover, setting goals contributes to overall well-being. When we have a sense of purpose and are actively working towards something meaningful, it boosts our self-esteem and satisfaction with life. It gives us a sense of accomplishment and fulfillment.

How to Identify Your Priorities and Values to Set Meaningful Goals

Before setting goals, it is crucial to identify our priorities and values. This step ensures that our goals align with what truly matters to us and increases the likelihood of achieving them.

One way to identify priorities and values is through journaling. Take some time to reflect on what brings you joy, fulfillment, and a sense of purpose. Write down your thoughts and feelings, and pay attention to recurring themes or patterns. This will help you gain clarity on what is most important to you.

Another strategy is self-reflection exercises. Engage in activities such as meditation, mindfulness, or deep introspection. These practices can help you connect with your inner self and uncover your core values and priorities.

It is also helpful to seek feedback from trusted friends or mentors. Sometimes, others can provide valuable insights and perspectives that we may not have considered ourselves.

The SMART Method: A Step-by-Step Guide to Setting Specific, Measurable, Achievable, Relevant, and Time-bound Goals

The SMART method is a popular framework for setting effective goals. It stands for Specific, Measurable, Achievable, Relevant, and Time-bound.

Specific goals are clear and well-defined. Instead of saying "I want to exercise more," a specific goal would be "I want to exercise for 30 minutes, three times a week."

Measurable goals have quantifiable criteria for success. For example, instead of saying "I want to save money," a measurable goal would be "I want to save $500 per month."

Achievable goals are realistic and within reach. It is important to set goals that challenge us but are still attainable. Setting unrealistic goals can lead to frustration and discouragement.

Relevant goals are aligned with our priorities and values. They should be meaningful and contribute to our overall well-being.

Time-bound goals have a specific deadline or timeframe attached to them. This helps create a sense of urgency and accountability. Instead of saying "I want to learn a new language," a time-bound goal would be "I want to learn conversational Spanish within six months."

By applying the SMART method to our goals, we increase the likelihood of success and ensure that our goals are well-defined and aligned with our priorities and values.

The Power of Visualization: How to Visualize Your Goals and Make Them a Reality

Visualization is a powerful technique that can help us achieve our goals. It involves creating vivid mental images of what we want to accomplish and experiencing the emotions associated with achieving those goals.

One way to visualize goals is by creating a vision board. A vision board is a collage of images, words, and quotes that represent our goals and aspirations. By looking at our vision board regularly, we reinforce our intentions and keep our goals at the forefront of our minds.

Another strategy is guided meditation. There are numerous guided meditations available that specifically focus on visualizing goals. These meditations guide us through the process of imagining ourselves achieving our goals and experiencing the emotions associated with that success.

Visualization helps us tap into the power of our subconscious mind. When we consistently visualize our goals, we program our minds to seek out opportunities and take actions that align with those goals. It increases our belief in ourselves and our ability to achieve what we desire.

Overcoming Obstacles and Staying Motivated: Tips and Strategies for Achieving Your Goals

While setting goals is important, it is equally crucial to anticipate and overcome obstacles that may arise along the way. Here are some tips and strategies for staying motivated and overcoming obstacles:

1. Break goals down into smaller tasks: Sometimes, big goals can feel overwhelming. By breaking them down into smaller, more manageable tasks, we can make progress and stay motivated.

2. Seek support from others: Surround yourself with people who support your goals and can provide encouragement and guidance when needed. Joining a mastermind group or finding an accountability partner can be beneficial.

3. Stay flexible: It is important to be adaptable and open to change. Circumstances may shift, and it is essential to adjust our goals and plans accordingly.

4. Practice self-care: Taking care of ourselves physically, mentally, and emotionally is crucial for staying motivated. Make sure to prioritize self-care activities such as exercise, rest, and relaxation.

5. Celebrate progress: Celebrating small wins along the way can boost motivation and provide a sense of accomplishment. Take time to acknowledge and reward yourself for the progress you have made.

The Role of Accountability in Goal Setting: How to Stay Accountable to Yourself and Others

Accountability plays a significant role in goal setting. When we hold ourselves accountable, we are more likely to stay committed and take consistent action towards our goals. Here are some tips for staying accountable:

1. Set deadlines: Assign specific deadlines to your goals and tasks. This creates a sense of urgency and helps you stay on track.

2. Share your goals with others: By sharing your goals with a trusted friend or mentor, you create a sense of external accountability. They can provide support, encouragement, and hold you accountable to your commitments.

3. Track your progress: Regularly monitor your progress towards your goals. This can be done through journaling, using a planner or tracking app, or setting regular check-ins with yourself or others.

4. Reflect on setbacks: If you encounter setbacks or obstacles, take the time to reflect on what went wrong and how you can learn from the experience. Use setbacks as opportunities for growth and improvement.

5. Be honest with yourself: It is important to be honest with yourself about your progress and efforts towards your goals. If you find yourself slacking or losing motivation, take the time to reassess and recommit to your goals.

Celebrating Small Wins: Why Celebrating Milestones Can Help You Stay Focused and Motivated

Celebrating small wins is an essential aspect of goal setting. It provides a sense of accomplishment, boosts motivation, and helps us stay focused on our long-term goals. Here are some tips for celebrating milestones:

1. Reward yourself: When you achieve a milestone or make significant progress towards your goals, reward yourself with something meaningful. It could be a small treat, a day off, or a special activity that brings you joy.

2. Reflect on accomplishments: Take the time to reflect on what you have achieved and how far you have come. Write down your accomplishments and express gratitude for your efforts.

3. Share your success: Share your achievements with others who have supported you along the way. Celebrate with friends, family, or colleagues who have been part of your journey.

4. Take a break: Sometimes, it is important to take a break and recharge. Celebrating milestones can involve taking time off to rest and rejuvenate before moving on to the next phase of your goals.

Celebrating small wins not only boosts motivation but also reinforces positive habits and behaviors that contribute to long-term success.

The Importance of Flexibility in Goal Setting: How to Adjust Your Goals as Circumstances Change

Flexibility is crucial in goal setting, especially in times of uncertainty and change. It is important to be adaptable and willing to adjust our goals as circumstances evolve. Here are some tips for maintaining flexibility:

1. Reevaluate priorities: Regularly reassess your priorities and values to ensure that your goals align with what is most important to you at any given time.

2. Set new deadlines: If circumstances change or unexpected events occur, be willing to adjust your deadlines or timelines accordingly. This allows for more realistic goal setting and reduces the likelihood of feeling overwhelmed or discouraged.

3. Seek feedback: Be open to feedback from trusted friends, mentors, or coaches. They can provide valuable insights and perspectives that may help you adjust your goals or approach.

4. Embrace change: Instead of resisting change, embrace it as an opportunity for growth and learning. Be willing to let go of goals that no longer serve you and embrace new opportunities that align with your evolving priorities.

Flexibility in goal setting allows us to adapt to changing circumstances and ensures that our goals remain relevant and meaningful.

Avoiding Burnout: How to Set Realistic Goals and Manage Your Time Effectively

Avoiding burnout is crucial for long-term success and well-being. Setting realistic goals and managing time effectively are essential strategies for preventing burnout. Here are some tips:

1. Set realistic goals: Be honest with yourself about what you can realistically achieve within a given timeframe. Setting overly ambitious goals can lead to burnout and disappointment.

2. Prioritize tasks: Identify the most important tasks that will contribute to your goals and focus on those first. This helps prevent overwhelm and ensures that you are allocating your time and energy effectively.

3. Delegate or outsource: If possible, delegate tasks or outsource certain responsibilities to free up your time and energy for more important activities.

4. Take breaks: Regularly schedule breaks throughout your day to rest, recharge, and prevent burnout. This could involve short breaks during work hours or longer breaks such as vacations or weekends off.

5. Practice self-care: Prioritize self-care activities such as exercise, rest, relaxation, and hobbies. Taking care of yourself physically, mentally, and emotionally is crucial for preventing burnout.

By setting realistic goals and managing your time effectively, you can maintain a healthy work-life balance and avoid burnout.

The Benefits of Tracking Your Progress: How to Monitor Your Success and Stay on Track

Tracking progress is an essential aspect of goal setting. It allows us to monitor our success, stay on track, and make adjustments as needed. Here are some tips for tracking progress:

1. Use a planner or journal: Write down your goals, tasks, and progress in a planner or journal. This provides a visual representation of your progress and helps you stay organized.

2. Set regular check-ins: Schedule regular check-ins with yourself to assess your progress towards your goals. This could be weekly, monthly, or quarterly, depending on the nature of your goals.

3. Celebrate milestones: As mentioned earlier, celebrating milestones is an important part of tracking progress. It provides motivation and reinforces positive habits and behaviors.

4. Seek feedback: Ask for feedback from trusted friends, mentors, or coaches. They can provide insights and perspectives that may help you adjust your goals or approach.

5. Adjust as needed: If you find that you are not making progress or encountering obstacles, be willing to adjust your goals or strategies. Flexibility is key in goal setting.

Tracking progress allows us to stay accountable, make adjustments when necessary, and maintain momentum towards our goals.

Putting It All Together: Creating a Personalized Action Plan for Achieving Your Goals in 2021

Now that we have explored various strategies for goal setting and achievement, it is time to put it all together and create a personalized action plan for achieving your goals in 2021. Here is a step-by-step guide:

1. Identify your priorities and values: Reflect on what is most important to you and what you want to achieve in the year ahead.

2. Set SMART goals: Use the SMART method to set specific, measurable, achievable, relevant, and time-bound goals that align with your priorities and values.

3. Visualize your goals: Create a vision board or engage in guided meditations to visualize your goals and reinforce your intentions.

4. Overcome obstacles and stay motivated: Develop strategies for overcoming obstacles and staying motivated, such as breaking goals down into smaller tasks and seeking support from others.

5. Stay accountable: Set deadlines, share your goals with others, track your progress, and reflect on setbacks to stay accountable to yourself and others.

6. Celebrate milestones: Celebrate small wins along the way to boost motivation and acknowledge your progress.

7. Be flexible: Be willing to adjust your goals and plans as circumstances change. Regularly reassess your priorities and values to ensure that your goals remain relevant and meaningful.

8. Avoid burnout: Set realistic goals, manage your time effectively, and prioritize self-care to prevent burnout.

9. Track your progress: Use a planner or journal, set regular check-ins, seek feedback, and make adjustments as needed to stay on track towards your goals.

10. Take action: Finally, take action and start working towards your goals. Break them down into actionable steps and commit to consistent effort and progress.

Setting goals is crucial for personal growth and success in 2021. It provides direction, motivation, and a sense of purpose. By identifying priorities and values, using the SMART method, visualizing goals, overcoming obstacles, staying accountable, celebrating milestones, embracing flexibility, avoiding burnout, tracking progress, and creating a personalized action plan, individuals can set meaningful goals and work towards achieving them in the year ahead. It is time to take action and make 2021 a year of growth and success.

Chapter 17: The Power of Connection: How Building a Support Network Can Change Your Life

Connection is a fundamental human need. We are social beings, wired for connection and belonging. From the moment we are born, we seek out relationships and connections with others. These connections provide us with a sense of support, validation, and love. They shape our identity and help us navigate the ups and downs of life.

The impact of isolation and loneliness on mental and physical health cannot be overstated. Research has shown that social isolation and loneliness can have detrimental effects on our well-being. It can lead to increased levels of stress, depression, anxiety, and even physical health problems such as high blood pressure and heart disease.

The Science of Connection: How Social Support Affects Our Health

Social support plays a crucial role in stress management and immune function. When we have strong social connections, we have a built-in support system that can help us cope with life's challenges. Whether it's a shoulder to cry on, someone to talk to, or someone to offer practical help, having people in our lives who care about us can make a world of difference.

On the other hand, social isolation has been linked to chronic illness. Studies have shown that individuals who lack social support are more likely to develop chronic conditions such as diabetes, heart disease, and even cancer. This may be due to the fact that social isolation can lead to unhealthy behaviors such as poor diet, lack of exercise, and substance abuse.

Building Your Support Network: Tips for Finding and Cultivating Relationships

Building a support network starts with identifying your needs and values in relationships. What qualities do you value in a friend or partner? What kind of support do you need? Once you have a clear understanding of what you're looking for, you can start seeking out opportunities to meet new people and build meaningful connections.

There are many strategies for meeting new people and building relationships. One approach is to join groups or organizations that align with your interests and values. This could be a sports team, a book club, or a volunteer organization. By engaging in activities that you enjoy, you are more likely to meet like-minded individuals who share your passions.

The Benefits of a Strong Support System: Emotional and Mental Health

Having a strong support system can have numerous benefits for your emotional and mental health. One of the key benefits is increased resilience and coping skills. When you have people in your life who support and believe in you, it can help you bounce back from setbacks and navigate difficult times with greater ease.

A strong support system can also improve your self-esteem and sense of belonging. When you have people who love and accept you for who you are, it can boost your self-confidence and help you feel like you belong. This sense of belonging is essential for our overall well-being and can contribute to greater happiness and life satisfaction.

How Connection Can Boost Your Career and Professional Development

Connection is not only important for our personal lives but also for our professional lives. Networking and mentorship play a crucial role in career development. By building relationships with others in your field, you can gain valuable insights, advice, and opportunities.

Supportive relationships also play a role in job satisfaction and success. When we feel supported by our colleagues and supervisors, we are more likely to be engaged in our work, perform at a higher level, and experience greater job satisfaction. Additionally, having a strong professional network can open doors to new opportunities and help advance your career.

The Role of Connection in Overcoming Life's Challenges and Obstacles

Life is full of challenges and obstacles, and having supportive relationships can make all the difference in overcoming them. When we face difficult times, having someone to lean on can provide us with the emotional support we need to keep going.

Shared experiences and empathy are powerful tools for overcoming challenges. When we connect with others who have gone through similar experiences, we can draw strength and inspiration from their stories. Additionally, having someone who understands and empathizes with our struggles can provide us with a sense of validation and comfort.

The Power of Vulnerability: How Sharing Your Struggles Can Strengthen Connections

Vulnerability is often seen as a weakness, but in reality, it is a strength. When we allow ourselves to be vulnerable and share our struggles with others, it can deepen our connections and foster intimacy.

Authenticity and trust are key components of strong relationships. When we are open and honest about our struggles, it creates a safe space for others to do the same. This vulnerability can lead to deeper connections and a greater sense of understanding and support.

The Impact of Community and Social Support on Addiction Recovery

Community and social support play a crucial role in addiction recovery. Support groups and peer networks provide individuals with a safe space to share their experiences, receive support, and learn from others who have been through similar struggles.

Having a sober social network is also important for maintaining sobriety. Surrounding yourself with people who support your recovery journey can help you stay on track and provide you with the encouragement and accountability you need.

Connection and Personal Growth: How Relationships Can Help You Reach Your Goals

Supportive relationships are not only important for overcoming challenges but also for personal growth. When we have people in our lives who believe in us and encourage us to reach our goals, it can fuel our motivation and drive.

Feedback and encouragement from others can also facilitate growth and change. When we receive constructive feedback from someone we trust, it can help us identify areas for improvement and push us to become the best version of ourselves.

Nurturing Connection in the Digital Age: Balancing Technology and Face-to-Face Interaction

In today's digital age, maintaining meaningful connections can be challenging. While technology has made it easier than ever to connect with others, it can also lead to feelings of isolation and disconnection.

Striking a balance between technology and face-to-face interaction is crucial. While social media and online communities can be a great way to stay connected, it's important to prioritize in-person interactions. Making time for quality face-to-face interactions can help foster deeper connections and combat feelings of loneliness and isolation.

The Enduring Power of Connection and the Importance of Prioritizing Relationships

In conclusion, connection is a fundamental human need that plays a crucial role in our well-being and success. The impact of supportive relationships on our mental, emotional, and physical health cannot be overstated.

Investing time and energy in cultivating and maintaining connections is essential. Whether it's building a support network, nurturing existing relationships, or seeking out new opportunities for connection, prioritizing relationships is an investment in our own happiness and well-being. So let's make an effort to reach out, connect, and build meaningful relationships that will enrich our lives for years to come.

Chapter 18: Breaking Down Barriers: Understanding the Benefits of Psychotherapy Techniques

Psychotherapy is a form of treatment that focuses on helping individuals overcome mental health issues and improve their overall well-being. It involves talking to a trained therapist who can provide support, guidance, and tools to help individuals navigate through their challenges. There are various psychotherapy techniques that can be used depending on the specific needs of the individual. It is important to address mental health concerns because they can have a significant impact on a person's quality of life and overall functioning.

The Importance of Addressing Mental Health Concerns

Mental health issues are more common than many people realize. According to the World Health Organization, approximately 1 in 4 people worldwide will experience a mental health issue at some point in their lives. In the United States alone, nearly 20% of adults experience a mental illness each year. These statistics highlight the prevalence of mental health concerns and the need for effective treatment.

Untreated mental health issues can have serious consequences. They can affect all aspects of a person's life, including their relationships, work performance, and physical health. Mental health issues can lead to feelings of isolation, hopelessness, and despair. They can also increase the risk of developing other health problems such as cardiovascular disease, diabetes, and substance abuse disorders. By addressing mental health concerns early on, individuals can prevent these negative outcomes and improve their overall well-being.

Understanding the Stigma Surrounding Psychotherapy

Despite the prevalence of mental health issues, there is still a significant stigma surrounding psychotherapy and seeking help for mental health concerns. Many people have misconceptions about psychotherapy and believe that it is only for individuals with severe mental illnesses or that it is a sign of weakness. This stigma can prevent individuals from seeking the help they need and can perpetuate feelings of shame and embarrassment.

The impact of stigma on seeking help for mental health concerns is significant. It can lead to delays in treatment, increased suffering, and a decreased quality of life. Stigma can also contribute to feelings of isolation and can prevent individuals from reaching out to their support networks for help. It is important to challenge these misconceptions and educate the public about the benefits of psychotherapy in order to break down the barriers to seeking help.

The Role of Psychotherapy in Breaking Down Barriers

Psychotherapy plays a crucial role in breaking down barriers to seeking help for mental health concerns. By providing a safe and non-judgmental space for individuals to explore their thoughts and feelings, psychotherapy can help reduce the stigma surrounding mental health issues. Therapists can also provide education and information about mental health, helping individuals understand that seeking help is a sign of strength rather than weakness.

In addition, psychotherapy can help individuals develop coping skills and strategies to manage their mental health concerns. This can empower individuals to take control of their own well-being and reduce their reliance on external sources of support. By providing individuals with the tools they need to navigate through their challenges, psychotherapy can help break down barriers and empower individuals to seek help.

Access to mental health care is another important factor in breaking down barriers to psychotherapy. Many individuals face barriers such as cost, lack of insurance coverage, and limited availability of mental health services. It is crucial that efforts are made to improve access to mental health care, particularly for marginalized populations who may face additional barriers such as discrimination and lack of cultural competence in the mental health system.

Common Psychotherapy Techniques and Their Benefits

There are various psychotherapy techniques that can be used to address different mental health concerns. These techniques are evidence-based and have been shown to be effective in treating a wide range of issues. Some common psychotherapy techniques include cognitive-behavioral therapy (CBT), dialectical behavioral therapy (DBT), eye movement desensitization and reprocessing (EMDR), mindfulness-based stress reduction (MBSR), and acceptance and commitment therapy (ACT).

Each of these techniques has its own unique benefits and can be tailored to meet the specific needs of the individual. For example, CBT focuses on identifying and changing negative thought patterns and behaviors that contribute to mental health issues such as anxiety and depression. DBT, on the other hand, is specifically designed to help individuals with borderline personality disorder develop skills to manage their emotions and improve their relationships.

Cognitive Behavioral Therapy (CBT) for Anxiety and Depression

Cognitive-behavioral therapy (CBT) is one of the most widely used psychotherapy techniques and has been shown to be effective in treating a variety of mental health issues, including anxiety and depression. CBT focuses on the connection between thoughts, feelings, and behaviors, and aims to help individuals identify and change negative thought patterns and behaviors that contribute to their symptoms.

In CBT, individuals work with a therapist to identify their negative thoughts and beliefs and challenge them with more realistic and positive alternatives. They also learn coping skills and strategies to manage their symptoms, such as relaxation techniques, problem-solving skills, and exposure therapy. By changing their thoughts and behaviors, individuals can reduce their symptoms of anxiety and depression and improve their overall well-being.

Dialectical Behavioral Therapy (DBT) for Borderline Personality Disorder

Dialectical behavioral therapy (DBT) is a specialized form of therapy that was originally developed to treat individuals with borderline personality disorder. It combines elements of cognitive-behavioral therapy (CBT) with mindfulness practices to help individuals develop skills to manage their emotions, improve their relationships, and reduce self-destructive behaviors.

In DBT, individuals learn skills such as mindfulness, distress tolerance, emotion regulation, and interpersonal effectiveness. These skills help individuals become more aware of their emotions, regulate their emotions in a healthy way, tolerate distressing situations, and communicate effectively with others. By developing these skills, individuals with borderline personality disorder can improve their overall functioning and quality of life.

Eye Movement Desensitization and Reprocessing (EMDR) for Trauma

Eye movement desensitization and reprocessing (EMDR) is a psychotherapy technique that is specifically designed to help individuals who have experienced trauma. It involves the use of bilateral stimulation, such as eye movements or tapping, while the individual recalls their traumatic memories. This bilateral stimulation helps the brain process the traumatic memories in a safe and controlled way, reducing the emotional distress associated with the memories.

EMDR also involves identifying and challenging negative beliefs that individuals may have about themselves as a result of the trauma. By replacing these negative beliefs with more positive and realistic ones, individuals can reduce their symptoms of post-traumatic stress disorder (PTSD) and improve their overall well-being.

Mindfulness-Based Stress Reduction (MBSR) for Stress and Anxiety

Mindfulness-based stress reduction (MBSR) is a psychotherapy technique that combines mindfulness practices with cognitive-behavioral therapy (CBT) to help individuals manage stress and anxiety. MBSR involves learning to pay attention to the present moment without judgment, which can help individuals become more aware of their thoughts, feelings, and bodily sensations.

In MBSR, individuals learn various mindfulness practices such as meditation, body scans, and mindful movement. These practices help individuals develop a greater sense of self-awareness and can reduce stress and anxiety by helping individuals stay grounded in the present moment rather than getting caught up in worries about the future or regrets about the past.

Acceptance and Commitment Therapy (ACT)

for Chronic Pain and Illness

Acceptance and commitment therapy (ACT) is a psychotherapy technique that focuses on helping individuals accept their thoughts and feelings rather than trying to change or control them. It is particularly effective for individuals with chronic pain and illness who may be struggling with the emotional and psychological impact of their condition.

In ACT, individuals learn to identify their values and commit to taking actions that are in line with those values, even in the presence of difficult thoughts and feelings. They also learn mindfulness practices to help them stay present and connected to the present moment, rather than getting caught up in worries about the future or regrets about the past. By accepting their thoughts and feelings and taking actions that are in line with their values, individuals can improve their overall well-being and quality of life.

The Importance of Seeking Help and Breaking Down Barriers to Psychotherapy

In conclusion, addressing mental health concerns is crucial for individuals to improve their overall well-being and quality of life. Psychotherapy plays a vital role in breaking down barriers to seeking help by providing a safe and non-judgmental space for individuals to explore their thoughts and feelings. By challenging misconceptions about psychotherapy and providing education about mental health, therapists can help reduce the stigma surrounding mental health issues.

There are various psychotherapy techniques that can be used to address different mental health concerns, such as cognitive-behavioral therapy (CBT), dialectical behavioral therapy (DBT), eye movement desensitization and reprocessing (EMDR), mindfulness-based stress reduction (MBSR), and acceptance and commitment therapy (ACT).

Each of these techniques has its own unique benefits and can be tailored to meet the specific needs of the individual.

It is important for individuals to seek help for their mental health concerns and break down barriers to psychotherapy. By doing so, they can improve their overall well-being, reduce their symptoms, and live a more fulfilling life. It is also important for society as a whole to support individuals in seeking help by improving access to mental health care and challenging the stigma surrounding mental health issues. Together, we can create a world where mental health is prioritized and individuals can get the help they need.

Chapter 19: Small Steps, Big Impact: How Lifestyle Changes Can Improve Your Health

Living a healthy lifestyle is crucial for overall health and well-being. Our daily habits and choices have a significant impact on our physical and mental health. Unhealthy habits such as poor diet, lack of exercise, inadequate sleep, and high stress levels can lead to a variety of health problems, including obesity, heart disease, diabetes, depression, and anxiety. On the other hand, making small lifestyle changes can have a big impact on our health and help prevent these diseases.

The Science behind Lifestyle Changes: How Small Steps Can Make a Big Impact

The science behind lifestyle changes lies in the concept of habit formation. Our brains are wired to seek pleasure and avoid pain, which is why we often find it difficult to make lasting changes. However, by understanding how habits are formed and using strategies to make them stick, we can make small but significant changes that lead to better health.

One effective strategy is to start with small steps. Instead of trying to overhaul your entire lifestyle overnight, focus on making one small change at a time. For example, if you want to incorporate exercise into your daily routine, start by taking a 10-minute walk every day. As this becomes a habit, gradually increase the duration and intensity of your workouts.

The Benefits of Regular Exercise: Boosting Physical and Mental Health

Regular exercise has numerous benefits for both physical and mental health. It helps maintain a healthy weight, reduces the risk of chronic diseases such as heart disease and diabetes, strengthens muscles and bones, improves cardiovascular health, and boosts immune function.

Exercise also has powerful effects on mental health. It releases endorphins, which are natural mood boosters that can help reduce symptoms of depression and anxiety. Exercise also improves sleep quality, increases self-confidence and body image, reduces stress levels, and enhances cognitive function.

To incorporate exercise into your daily routine, find activities that you enjoy and make them a priority. This could be anything from walking, jogging, swimming, dancing, or playing a sport. Aim for at least 150 minutes of moderate-intensity exercise or 75 minutes of vigorous-intensity exercise per week.

Healthy Eating Habits: The Key to a Balanced Diet and Improved Well-being

Eating a healthy diet is essential for overall health and well-being. A balanced diet provides the necessary nutrients, vitamins, and minerals that our bodies need to function properly. It can help prevent chronic diseases, maintain a healthy weight, boost energy levels, improve digestion, and enhance mental clarity.

To make healthier food choices, focus on incorporating more fruits, vegetables, whole grains, lean proteins, and healthy fats into your diet. Limit your intake of processed foods, sugary drinks, and foods high in saturated fats and sodium.

Meal planning and preparation can also help you make healthier choices. Plan your meals ahead of time, make a grocery list, and cook meals in bulk to have healthy options readily available throughout the week. It's also important to listen to your body's hunger and fullness cues and eat mindfully.

The Role of Sleep in Health: Tips for Getting a Better Night's Rest

Sleep plays a crucial role in our physical and mental health. It is during sleep that our bodies repair and regenerate cells, consolidate memories, regulate hormones, and restore energy levels. Lack of sleep or poor sleep quality can lead to a variety of health problems, including obesity, diabetes, heart disease, depression, and impaired cognitive function.

To improve sleep quality, establish a consistent sleep schedule by going to bed and waking up at the same time every day. Create a relaxing bedtime routine that includes activities such as reading a book, taking a warm bath, or practicing relaxation techniques like deep breathing or meditation. Make your bedroom a sleep-friendly environment by keeping it cool, dark, and quiet. Avoid electronic devices and stimulating activities before bed, as they can interfere with sleep.

Reducing Stress: Simple Strategies for Managing Stress and Anxiety

Stress is a normal part of life, but chronic stress can have a detrimental effect on our health. It can lead to a variety of physical and mental health problems, including high blood pressure, heart disease, obesity, depression, and anxiety. Therefore, it is important to find effective strategies for managing stress and promoting relaxation.

One effective strategy is to engage in stress-reducing activities such as exercise, meditation, deep breathing exercises, yoga, or spending time in nature. These activities help activate the body's relaxation response and reduce the production of stress hormones.

It is also important to prioritize self-care and make time for activities that bring you joy and relaxation. This could be anything from reading a book, listening to music, taking a bath, practicing a hobby, or spending time with loved ones. Additionally, learning to manage your time effectively and setting realistic goals can help reduce stress levels.

The Dangers of Smoking: How Quitting Can Improve Your Health

Smoking is one of the leading causes of preventable diseases and premature death worldwide. It is responsible for numerous health problems, including lung cancer, heart disease, stroke, respiratory infections, and chronic obstructive pulmonary disease (COPD). Quitting smoking is one of the best things you can do for your health.

There are many resources available to help you quit smoking. Nicotine replacement therapy (NRT), such as nicotine patches or gum, can help reduce withdrawal symptoms. Prescription medications such as bupropion or varenicline can also be effective in helping you quit smoking.

In addition to seeking professional help, it is important to build a support system of friends and family who can provide encouragement and accountability. Find healthy ways to cope with cravings and manage stress, such as engaging in physical activity, practicing relaxation techniques, or seeking support from a therapist or counselor.

The Importance of Hydration: Staying Hydrated for Better Health

Staying hydrated is essential for overall health and well-being. Water is involved in numerous bodily functions, including digestion, absorption, circulation, and temperature regulation. It helps maintain healthy skin, lubricates joints, flushes out toxins, and aids in weight management.

To stay hydrated, aim to drink at least 8 cups (64 ounces) of water per day. However, individual needs may vary depending on factors such as age, activity level, climate, and overall health. It is also important to listen to your body's thirst cues and drink water throughout the day.

If you struggle to drink enough water, try infusing it with fruits or herbs for added flavor. Carry a reusable water bottle with you wherever you go as a reminder to stay hydrated. You can also incorporate hydrating foods into your diet, such as fruits and vegetables with high water content.

The Power of Mindfulness: How Being Present Can Improve Your Mental Health

Mindfulness is the practice of being fully present in the moment and non-judgmentally aware of one's thoughts, feelings, and sensations. It has been shown to have numerous benefits for mental health, including reducing stress and anxiety, improving focus and attention, enhancing self-awareness and emotional regulation, and promoting overall well-being.

To incorporate mindfulness into your daily routine, start by setting aside a few minutes each day for formal mindfulness practice. This could be sitting quietly and focusing on your breath, practicing a body scan meditation, or engaging in mindful movement such as yoga or tai chi.

In addition to formal practice, you can also incorporate mindfulness into everyday activities. For example, when eating a meal, pay attention to the taste, texture, and smell of the food. When walking outside, notice the sensations of your feet touching the ground and the sounds and sights around you. By bringing awareness to the present moment, you can cultivate a sense of calm and reduce stress and anxiety.

Social Connections and Health: The Benefits of Building Strong Relationships

Social connections play a vital role in our health and well-being. Research has shown that people with strong social support networks have better physical and mental health outcomes, lower rates of chronic diseases, and longer life expectancy.

Building and maintaining strong relationships can be beneficial for your health. Make an effort to connect with friends, family, and loved ones on a regular basis. This could be through phone calls, video chats, or in-person meetings. Joining clubs, organizations, or community groups can also provide opportunities to meet new people and build social connections.

It is important to prioritize quality over quantity when it comes to relationships. Surround yourself with people who uplift and support you, and who share similar values and interests. Be a good listener and offer support to others when they need it. By nurturing your social connections, you can improve your overall health and well-being.

Taking Small Steps for a Healthier, Happier Life

In conclusion, making small lifestyle changes can have a big impact on our health and well-being. By incorporating regular exercise, healthy eating habits, adequate sleep, stress management techniques, quitting smoking, staying hydrated, practicing mindfulness, and building strong social connections into our daily routines, we can improve our physical and mental health.

It is important to remember that change takes time and effort. Start by making one small change at a time and gradually build upon it. Celebrate your successes along the way and be kind to yourself if you slip up. Remember that every small step towards a healthier lifestyle is a step in the right direction.

By prioritizing your health and making conscious choices that support your well-being, you can live a healthier, happier life. Take control of your habits and make the commitment to make small lifestyle changes today. Your body and mind will thank you for it.

Chapter 20: The Power of Self-Love: A Key to Empowerment

Self-love is a concept that has gained significant attention in recent years, and for good reason. It is the foundation of personal growth and well-being, and it plays a crucial role in our overall happiness and success. In this article, we will explore the importance of self-love and its impact on various aspects of our lives. From empowerment and confidence to mental health and resilience, self-love has the power to transform our lives for the better.

Understanding the Importance of Self-Love

Self-love can be defined as the practice of nurturing and caring for oneself, both physically and emotionally. It involves accepting ourselves as we are, flaws and all, and treating ourselves with kindness, compassion, and respect. Self-love is not about being selfish or narcissistic; rather, it is about recognizing our own worth and valuing ourselves as deserving of love and happiness.

Self-love is important for personal growth and well-being because it allows us to develop a positive relationship with ourselves. When we love ourselves, we are more likely to make choices that align with our values and goals. We are also more likely to set healthy boundaries, prioritize self-care, and engage in activities that bring us joy and fulfillment. Self-love provides a solid foundation for personal growth, as it allows us to build a strong sense of self-worth and confidence.

The Connection Between Self-Love and Empowerment

Self-love is closely linked to empowerment because it gives individuals the power to take control of their lives. When we love ourselves, we believe in our own abilities and have faith in our capacity to overcome challenges. This belief in ourselves empowers us to make decisions that align with our values and goals, rather than seeking validation or approval from others.

Self-love also leads to greater self-efficacy, which is the belief in our ability to succeed in specific situations or accomplish specific tasks. When we love ourselves, we trust in our own abilities and have confidence in our skills and talents. This self-efficacy allows us to take risks, pursue our passions, and achieve our goals. Without self-love, we may doubt ourselves and hold back from pursuing our dreams, limiting our potential for growth and success.

How Self-Love Boosts Confidence

Self-love is a powerful tool for boosting confidence and improving self-esteem. When we love ourselves, we recognize our own worth and value, which in turn leads to a positive self-image. We are able to see ourselves as deserving of love, respect, and success, which boosts our confidence in all areas of life.

Self-love also helps us overcome self-doubt and negative self-talk. When we love ourselves, we are kind and compassionate towards ourselves, even when we make mistakes or face challenges. We are able to reframe negative thoughts and replace them with positive affirmations. This positive self-talk builds our confidence and allows us to approach life with a sense of optimism and resilience.

The Science Behind Self-Love and Its Impact on Mental Health

Research has shown that self-love has a significant impact on mental health. When we practice self-love, we experience lower levels of stress and anxiety, as well as improved overall well-being. This is because self-love involves taking care of ourselves physically, emotionally, and mentally.

Self-love reduces stress by helping us prioritize self-care and set boundaries. When we love ourselves, we recognize the importance of taking time for ourselves and engaging in activities that bring us joy and relaxation. This self-care helps us recharge and rejuvenate, reducing stress levels and improving our mental health.

Additionally, self-love improves overall well-being by fostering a positive mindset. When we love ourselves, we are more likely to focus on the positive aspects of our lives and practice gratitude. This positive mindset has been linked to improved mental health and greater life satisfaction.

The Role of Self-Love in Building Resilience

Resilience is the ability to bounce back from setbacks and challenges, and self-love plays a crucial role in developing this resilience. When we love ourselves, we are able to view failures and setbacks as opportunities for growth and learning, rather than as reflections of our worth or abilities.

Self-love also helps us develop a growth mindset, which is the belief that our abilities and intelligence can be developed through effort and practice. When we love ourselves, we believe in our own potential for growth and success, even in the face of adversity. This belief in ourselves allows us to persevere through challenges and bounce back stronger than before.

Strategies for Cultivating Self-Love

Cultivating self-love is a lifelong journey, but there are practical strategies that can help us develop a stronger sense of self-love. One strategy is practicing self-compassion, which involves treating ourselves with kindness and understanding, especially during difficult times. This means acknowledging our mistakes and shortcomings without judgment, and offering ourselves the same compassion we would offer to a loved one.

Setting boundaries is another important strategy for cultivating self-love. When we set boundaries, we prioritize our own needs and well-being, which is an act of self-love. This means saying no when necessary, and not overextending ourselves to please others. Setting boundaries allows us to protect our energy and focus on activities that bring us joy and fulfillment.

Incorporating self-love into our daily routines is also essential for cultivating self-love. This can include engaging in activities that bring us joy, such as hobbies or spending time with loved ones. It can also involve practicing self-care rituals, such as taking baths, meditating, or journaling. By making self-love a priority in our daily lives, we reinforce the importance of self-love and strengthen our relationship with ourselves.

Overcoming Self-Doubt: The Power of Self-Love

Self-doubt is a common obstacle that many individuals face, but self-love has the power to overcome this self-doubt. When we love ourselves, we recognize our own worth and value, which allows us to challenge negative thoughts and beliefs about ourselves.

Self-love helps us develop a more positive self-image by focusing on our strengths and accomplishments. When we love ourselves, we are able to see ourselves as capable and deserving of success, which helps us overcome self-doubt and pursue our goals with confidence.

The Relationship Between Self-Love and Self-Care

Self-love and self-care are interconnected because self-love involves prioritizing our own needs and well-being. When we love ourselves, we recognize the importance of taking care of ourselves physically, emotionally, and mentally.

Self-care is an act of self-love because it involves engaging in activities that bring us joy, relaxation, and rejuvenation. This can include activities such as exercise, spending time in nature, practicing mindfulness or meditation, or engaging in creative pursuits. By prioritizing self-care, we reinforce our own worth and value, and strengthen our relationship with ourselves.

How Self-Love Can Improve Relationships

Self-love not only improves our relationship with ourselves but also has a positive impact on our relationships with others. When we love ourselves, we are able to set healthy boundaries and communicate effectively with others.

Setting healthy boundaries is an act of self-love because it allows us to protect our energy and prioritize our own needs. By setting boundaries, we communicate to others what is acceptable and what is not, which leads to healthier and more fulfilling relationships.

Effective communication is also a result of self-love because when we love ourselves, we are able to express our needs, desires, and feelings in a clear and assertive manner. This allows us to build deeper connections with others and foster healthier relationships.

The Link Between Self-Love and Success

Self-love is closely linked to success in various areas of life. When we love ourselves, we believe in our own abilities and have confidence in our skills and talents. This belief in ourselves allows us to pursue our goals with determination and resilience, increasing our chances of success.

Self-love also helps us overcome fear of failure and take risks. When we love ourselves, we recognize that failure is a natural part of the learning process and an opportunity for growth. This mindset allows us to step outside of our comfort zones and pursue new opportunities, which can lead to greater success.

The Long-Term Benefits of Prioritizing Self-Love

Prioritizing self-love has numerous long-term benefits that extend beyond personal growth and well-being. By practicing self-love, we improve our mental health, develop greater resilience, and strengthen our relationships with ourselves and others.

Improved mental health is a significant long-term benefit of self-love. When we prioritize self-love, we reduce stress levels, improve overall well-being, and develop a positive mindset. This leads to improved mental health and greater life satisfaction.

Greater resilience is another long-term benefit of self-love. When we love ourselves, we are able to bounce back from setbacks and challenges with greater ease. This resilience allows us to navigate through life's ups and downs with grace and strength.

In conclusion, self-love is a powerful force that has the ability to transform our lives for the better. By understanding the importance of self-love and implementing strategies for cultivating it, we can experience greater empowerment, confidence, mental health, resilience, and success. It is essential that we prioritize self-love in our daily lives in order to reap the long-term benefits and live a life filled with happiness and fulfillment.

Chapter 21: Breaking the Cycle: Effective Strategies for Relapse Prevention

Relapse prevention is a crucial aspect of addiction recovery. It involves understanding the nature of relapse, identifying triggers and high-risk situations, developing coping skills and strategies, building a support system, practicing mindfulness and self-awareness, setting realistic goals and expectations, creating a healthy lifestyle, addressing co-occurring mental health issues, seeking professional help and treatment, learning from past mistakes and failures, and celebrating success and progress. By implementing these strategies, individuals in recovery can increase their chances of maintaining long-term sobriety.

Understanding the Nature of Relapse

Relapse is defined as the recurrence of substance use after a period of abstinence. It is important to understand that relapse is not a sign of failure or weakness, but rather a common part of the recovery process. Relapse typically occurs in stages, starting with emotional relapse, where individuals may experience negative emotions and thoughts that can lead to cravings. This can then progress to mental relapse, where individuals may start to romanticize their past substance use and consider using again. Finally, physical relapse occurs when individuals actually engage in substance use.

There are several common misconceptions about relapse that need to be addressed. One misconception is that relapse is inevitable and cannot be prevented. While relapse rates are high for individuals in recovery, it is important to remember that many people do achieve long-term sobriety. Another misconception is that relapse occurs suddenly and without warning. In reality, there are often warning signs and triggers that can be identified and addressed before a relapse occurs.

Identifying Triggers and High-Risk Situations

Triggers are people, places, things, or situations that can increase the risk of relapse. Common triggers include stress, negative emotions, social situations where substances are present, and exposure to cues associated with past substance use. It is important for individuals in recovery to be self-aware and identify their personal triggers. This can be done through reflection, journaling, and seeking feedback from others.

Once triggers have been identified, it is important to develop strategies for avoiding or managing them. For example, if stress is a trigger, individuals can practice stress management techniques such as deep breathing, exercise, or engaging in a hobby. If social situations where substances are present are a trigger, individuals can avoid these situations or bring a sober support person with them. By being proactive and prepared, individuals can reduce their risk of relapse.

Developing Coping Skills and Strategies

Developing healthy coping skills is essential for relapse prevention. Many individuals turn to substances as a way to cope with stress, negative emotions, or other challenges. By developing alternative coping strategies, individuals can reduce their reliance on substances and increase their ability to handle difficult situations.

There are many coping strategies that can be effective in addiction recovery. Mindfulness is one technique that involves being fully present in the moment and non-judgmentally observing one's thoughts and feelings. This can help individuals become more aware of their triggers and cravings and make conscious choices about how to respond to them. Other coping strategies include exercise, which can release endorphins and improve mood, and journaling, which can provide an outlet for emotions and thoughts.

It is important for individuals in recovery to create a personalized relapse prevention plan that includes a variety of coping skills and strategies. This plan should be flexible and adaptable to different situations and should be regularly reviewed and updated as needed.

Building a Support System

Having a strong support system is crucial for relapse prevention. Recovery can be challenging, and having people who understand and support you can make a significant difference. There are many types of support available, including 12-step programs such as Alcoholics Anonymous or Narcotics Anonymous, therapy with a licensed professional, and sober living homes.

Building a support system involves reaching out to others and being open and honest about your struggles and needs. This can be difficult for some individuals, especially if they have experienced judgment or rejection in the past. However, it is important to remember that there are people who want to help and support you in your recovery journey.

Maintaining a support system requires ongoing effort and communication. It is important to attend meetings or therapy sessions regularly, reach out to others when you need support, and be willing to offer support to others in return. By building and maintaining a strong support system, individuals can increase their chances of long-term sobriety.

Practicing Mindfulness and Self-Awareness

Mindfulness is a practice that involves paying attention to the present moment without judgment. It can be a powerful tool in addiction recovery because it helps individuals become more aware of their thoughts, feelings, and physical sensations. By practicing mindfulness, individuals can become more attuned to their triggers and cravings and make conscious choices about how to respond to them.

There are many ways to practice mindfulness, including meditation, deep breathing exercises, and body scans. Meditation involves sitting quietly and focusing on the breath or a specific object or mantra. Deep breathing exercises involve taking slow, deep breaths in through the nose and out through the mouth. Body scans involve systematically bringing attention to different parts of the body and noticing any sensations or tension.

Practicing mindfulness requires regular effort and commitment. It can be helpful to set aside dedicated time each day for mindfulness practice, but it is also important to incorporate mindfulness into everyday activities. For example, individuals can practice mindful eating by paying attention to the taste, texture, and smell of their food.

Setting Realistic Goals and Expectations

Setting realistic goals is important for maintaining motivation and focus in addiction recovery. It is easy to become overwhelmed or discouraged if goals are too ambitious or unrealistic. By setting achievable goals, individuals can experience a sense of accomplishment and progress, which can help maintain motivation and momentum.

When setting goals, it is important to be specific, measurable, achievable, relevant, and time-bound (SMART). For example, instead of setting a vague goal like "get healthy," a SMART goal might be "exercise for 30 minutes three times per week for the next month." This goal is specific (exercise for 30 minutes), measurable (three times per week), achievable (based on individual capabilities), relevant (related to getting healthy), and time-bound (for the next month).

Staying focused on goals requires ongoing effort and commitment. It can be helpful to break larger goals into smaller, more manageable steps and to regularly review and revise goals as needed. By setting realistic goals and expectations, individuals can increase their chances of long-term success in recovery.

Creating a Healthy Lifestyle

Creating a healthy lifestyle is essential for relapse prevention. Substance use often takes a toll on physical and mental health, so it is important to prioritize self-care and engage in activities that promote overall well-being. This includes exercise, nutrition, sleep, and stress management.

Exercise has been shown to have numerous benefits for individuals in recovery, including reducing cravings, improving mood, and increasing overall well-being. It is important to find activities that are enjoyable and sustainable, whether it's going for a walk, practicing yoga, or playing a team sport.

Nutrition is also important for recovery. A balanced diet that includes fruits, vegetables, whole grains, lean proteins, and healthy fats can provide the nutrients needed for optimal physical and mental health. It is important to avoid skipping meals or relying on processed or sugary foods as a way to cope with cravings or emotions.

Sleep is often disrupted during active addiction, so establishing healthy sleep habits is crucial in recovery. This includes maintaining a consistent sleep schedule, creating a relaxing bedtime routine, and creating a sleep-friendly environment.

Stress management is another important aspect of a healthy lifestyle. Chronic stress can increase the risk of relapse, so it is important to find healthy ways to cope with stress. This can include practicing relaxation techniques such as deep breathing or meditation, engaging in hobbies or activities that bring joy, and seeking support from others.

Addressing Co-Occurring Mental Health Issues

Many individuals with addiction also have co-occurring mental health issues, such as depression, anxiety, or trauma-related disorders. These mental health issues can contribute to substance use and increase the risk of relapse. It is important to address these issues in recovery in order to achieve long-term sobriety.

Addressing co-occurring disorders often involves a combination of therapy and medication. Therapy can help individuals develop coping skills, process past trauma, and address underlying issues that contribute to substance use. Medication-assisted treatment may also be recommended for individuals with certain mental health conditions, such as depression or anxiety.

It is important to work with a qualified professional to develop an individualized treatment plan that addresses both addiction and mental health issues. By addressing co-occurring disorders, individuals can improve their overall well-being and reduce the risk of relapse.

Seeking Professional Help and Treatment

Professional help and treatment are essential for individuals in addiction recovery. While some individuals are able to achieve sobriety on their own, many benefit from the support and guidance of professionals who specialize in addiction treatment.

There are many types of treatment available, including therapy, medication-assisted treatment, detoxification, and residential or outpatient programs. Therapy can help individuals develop coping skills, address underlying issues, and learn relapse prevention strategies. Medication-assisted treatment involves the use of medications to reduce cravings and withdrawal symptoms. Detoxification is the process of safely removing substances from the body under medical supervision. Residential or outpatient programs provide structured support and education for individuals in recovery.

Finding and accessing professional help and treatment can be challenging, but it is important to reach out for support. This can involve contacting local treatment centers, speaking with a primary care physician, or reaching out to a helpline or support group. By seeking professional help and treatment, individuals can increase their chances of successful recovery.

Learning from Past Mistakes and Failures

Learning from past mistakes and failures is an important part of the recovery process. It is common for individuals in recovery to experience setbacks or relapses, but it is important to view these experiences as learning opportunities rather than as signs of failure.

Reflecting on past experiences can help individuals identify patterns, triggers, and warning signs that may have contributed to relapse. This can involve journaling, talking with a therapist or support group, or seeking feedback from trusted friends or family members. By understanding what went wrong in the past, individuals can make changes and develop strategies to prevent future relapses.

It is also important to avoid repeating past mistakes. This may involve making changes to one's environment, such as avoiding places or people associated with substance use. It may also involve developing new coping skills or seeking additional support. By learning from past mistakes and failures, individuals can increase their chances of long-term sobriety.

Celebrating Success and Progress

Celebrating success and progress is an important part of the recovery journey. Recovery can be challenging, and it is important to acknowledge and celebrate milestones and achievements along the way. This can help maintain motivation and momentum and provide a sense of accomplishment and pride.

There are many ways to celebrate success in recovery. This can include treating oneself to something special, such as a favorite meal or activity. It can also involve sharing achievements with others, such as attending a support group meeting or therapy session and sharing progress. By celebrating success, individuals can stay motivated and focused on their recovery goals.

Relapse prevention is a crucial aspect of addiction recovery. By understanding the nature of relapse, identifying triggers and high-risk situations, developing coping skills and strategies, building a support system, practicing mindfulness and self-awareness, setting realistic goals and expectations, creating a healthy lifestyle, addressing co-occurring mental health issues, seeking professional help and treatment, learning from past mistakes and failures, and celebrating success and progress, individuals can increase their chances of maintaining long-term sobriety. Recovery is a lifelong journey, and it requires ongoing effort and commitment. However, with the right strategies and support, individuals can achieve a successful recovery.

Chapter 22: Finding Your Voice: How Creative Expression Can Help You Discover Your True Self

Finding your voice is an essential part of personal growth and self-discovery. It is about understanding who you truly are, what you believe in, and what you want to express to the world. When you find your voice, you gain a sense of authenticity and confidence that can positively impact all areas of your life.

One powerful tool for finding your voice is creative expression. Whether it's through writing, art, music, or dance, creative expression allows you to tap into your innermost thoughts and emotions, helping you discover your true self. By engaging in creative activities, you can explore different aspects of your identity and uncover hidden talents and passions.

Understanding the Importance of Self-Discovery for Personal Growth

Self-discovery is a journey of exploration and introspection that leads to personal growth. It involves gaining a deeper understanding of yourself, your values, and your purpose in life. When you embark on a journey of self-discovery, you open yourself up to new possibilities and experiences that can shape your identity and help you become the best version of yourself.

Self-discovery is important for personal growth because it allows you to align your actions with your values and passions. When you know who you are and what you stand for, you can make choices that are in line with your authentic self. This leads to a greater sense of fulfillment and happiness in life.

The Relationship between Creative Expression and Self-Discovery

Creative expression is closely linked to self-discovery because it provides a means for exploring and expressing your innermost thoughts and emotions. Through creative activities, you can tap into your subconscious mind and uncover aspects of yourself that may have been hidden or suppressed.

Creative expression allows you to break free from societal expectations and express yourself authentically. It gives you the freedom to explore different aspects of your identity without judgment or fear of rejection. By engaging in creative activities, you can gain a deeper understanding of who you are and what you want to communicate to the world.

Exploring Different Forms of Creative Expression for Self-Discovery

There are many different forms of creative expression that can aid in self-discovery. Some popular forms include writing, art, music, and dance. Each form offers a unique way to explore your thoughts, emotions, and desires.

Writing is a powerful tool for self-discovery because it allows you to reflect on your experiences and express your thoughts and feelings in a structured manner. Through writing, you can gain clarity on your values, beliefs, and goals, helping you find your voice.

Art, whether it's painting, drawing, or sculpting, allows you to tap into your creativity and express yourself visually. It can be a cathartic process that helps you process emotions and gain insight into your inner world.

Music and dance are forms of creative expression that engage both the mind and body. They allow you to express yourself through movement and rhythm, helping you connect with your emotions and find your voice.

How Writing Can Help You Discover Your Voice and Uncover Your True Self

Writing is a powerful tool for self-discovery because it allows you to explore your thoughts and emotions in a structured manner. Through writing, you can gain clarity on your values, beliefs, and goals, helping you find your voice.

When you write, you have the opportunity to reflect on your experiences and express yourself authentically. You can explore different perspectives and gain insight into your own thoughts and feelings. Writing also allows you to experiment with different writing styles and genres, helping you discover what resonates with you the most.

Writing can also be a form of therapy. It allows you to release pent-up emotions and process difficult experiences. By putting your thoughts and feelings onto paper, you can gain a sense of closure and healing.

The Healing Power of Art Therapy in Finding Your Voice

Art therapy is a form of creative expression that combines the benefits of art and therapy. It is a powerful tool for self-discovery and healing, as it allows you to express yourself visually and process emotions in a safe and supportive environment.

Art therapy can help you find your voice by providing a means for exploring and expressing your innermost thoughts and emotions. Through art-making, you can tap into your subconscious mind and uncover aspects of yourself that may have been hidden or suppressed.

Art therapy also provides a non-verbal form of communication, allowing you to express emotions that may be difficult to put into words. By creating art, you can gain insight into your own thoughts and feelings, helping you find your voice.

Discovering Your True Self through Music and Dance

Music and dance are powerful forms of creative expression that engage both the mind and body. They allow you to express yourself through movement and rhythm, helping you connect with your emotions and find your voice.

Music has the ability to evoke strong emotions and memories. By listening to music that resonates with you, you can tap into your own thoughts and feelings, helping you gain insight into your true self.

Dance is a physical expression of emotion. By moving your body to the rhythm of music, you can release pent-up emotions and connect with your innermost self. Dance allows you to express yourself authentically and find your voice through movement.

The Role of Mindfulness in Creative Expression and Self-Discovery

Mindfulness is the practice of being fully present in the moment, without judgment or attachment. It is an important aspect of creative expression and self-discovery because it allows you to fully engage with the creative process and connect with your true self.

When you engage in creative activities mindfully, you are able to fully immerse yourself in the experience. This allows you to tap into your intuition and express yourself authentically. By being present in the moment, you can gain insight into your own thoughts and feelings, helping you find your voice.

Mindfulness also helps you overcome self-doubt and fear in the creative process. By staying present and focused, you can let go of judgment and perfectionism, allowing your true self to shine through.

Overcoming Fear and Resistance in the Creative Process

Fear and resistance are common obstacles in the creative process. They can prevent you from fully expressing yourself and finding your voice. However, with awareness and practice, you can overcome these obstacles and tap into your true creative potential.

One way to overcome fear and resistance is to acknowledge and accept them. By recognizing that fear and resistance are natural parts of the creative process, you can let go of judgment and perfectionism. This allows you to embrace vulnerability and take risks in your creative expression.

Another way to overcome fear and resistance is to cultivate a supportive environment. Surround yourself with people who encourage and inspire you. Seek out feedback and constructive criticism from trusted individuals who can help you grow as an artist.

Embracing Vulnerability and Authenticity in Creative Expression

Vulnerability and authenticity are key elements of creative expression. They allow you to express yourself honestly and connect with your true self. By embracing vulnerability and authenticity, you can find your voice and create meaningful art.

To embrace vulnerability in your creative expression, it's important to let go of judgment and perfectionism. Allow yourself to take risks and make mistakes. Embrace the imperfections in your art as a reflection of your unique voice.

Authenticity comes from being true to yourself and expressing your own thoughts and feelings. Avoid comparing yourself to others or trying to imitate their style. Instead, focus on expressing what is true for you.

Finding Your Voice and Embracing Your True Self through Creative Expression

Creative expression is a powerful tool for self-discovery and personal growth. It allows you to tap into your innermost thoughts and emotions, helping you find your voice and embrace your true self.

By engaging in different forms of creative expression, such as writing, art, music, and dance, you can explore different aspects of your identity and uncover hidden talents and passions. Through creative activities, you can gain a deeper understanding of who you are and what you want to communicate to the world.

So, don't be afraid to explore different forms of creative expression and embark on a journey of self-discovery. Find your voice and embrace your true self through the power of creative expression.

Chapter 23: The Power of Mindfulness: How to Find Inner Peace and Happiness

Mindfulness is a practice that has gained significant popularity in recent years, as people seek ways to find peace and balance in their fast-paced lives. In today's world, where we are constantly bombarded with distractions and demands, mindfulness offers a way to slow down, be present, and cultivate a sense of inner calm. This article will explore the concept of mindfulness, its benefits, and how it can help us find inner peace and happiness.

Understanding the Concept of Mindfulness

Mindfulness can be defined as the practice of intentionally paying attention to the present moment without judgment. It involves bringing our awareness to our thoughts, feelings, bodily sensations, and the environment around us. The roots of mindfulness can be traced back to ancient Eastern traditions such as Buddhism, where it was used as a tool for spiritual growth and enlightenment.

There are various types of mindfulness practices, including meditation, breathing exercises, and body scans. Meditation involves sitting in a quiet space and focusing on the breath or a specific object of attention. Breathing exercises involve consciously observing and regulating our breath to bring about a state of relaxation. Body scans involve systematically bringing our attention to different parts of the body to cultivate awareness and relaxation.

The Benefits of Practicing Mindfulness

Practicing mindfulness has been shown to have numerous physical, mental, and emotional benefits. On a physical level, mindfulness can help reduce stress levels, lower blood pressure, improve sleep quality, and boost the immune system. It can also help manage chronic pain and improve overall physical well-being.

On a mental level, mindfulness can enhance cognitive function, improve focus and concentration, increase self-awareness, and reduce rumination and negative thinking patterns. It can also help manage symptoms of anxiety and depression and improve overall mental well-being.

Emotionally, mindfulness can help regulate emotions, increase self-compassion and empathy towards others, and improve overall emotional well-being. It can also help cultivate a sense of gratitude and contentment, leading to greater happiness and fulfillment.

How Mindfulness Helps in Finding Inner Peace

Inner peace can be defined as a state of calmness, tranquility, and harmony within oneself. It is a state of being where one feels grounded, centered, and at ease, regardless of external circumstances. Mindfulness can help us find inner peace by bringing our attention to the present moment and cultivating a non-judgmental attitude towards our thoughts and emotions.

By practicing mindfulness, we learn to observe our thoughts and emotions without getting caught up in them or reacting impulsively. We develop the ability to step back and create space between ourselves and our thoughts, allowing us to respond to situations with greater clarity and wisdom. This sense of detachment from our thoughts and emotions allows us to experience a sense of inner peace and freedom.

Many individuals have found inner peace through the practice of mindfulness. They have reported feeling more grounded, centered, and at ease in their daily lives. They have experienced a greater sense of acceptance and contentment, even in the face of challenges and difficulties. By cultivating mindfulness, they have been able to find a deep sense of peace within themselves.

Mindfulness Techniques to Achieve Inner Peace

There are various mindfulness techniques that can help us achieve inner peace. One such technique is breathing exercises, where we focus on our breath as a way to anchor ourselves in the present moment. By bringing our attention to the sensations of the breath entering and leaving our body, we can cultivate a sense of calmness and relaxation.

Another technique is body scan meditation, where we systematically bring our attention to different parts of the body, starting from the top of the head down to the toes. This practice helps us develop awareness of bodily sensations and release tension or discomfort that may be present.

Mindful walking is another technique that can help us find inner peace. By bringing our attention to the sensations of walking, such as the feeling of the ground beneath our feet or the movement of our legs, we can cultivate a sense of groundedness and presence.

Loving-kindness meditation is a practice that involves cultivating feelings of love, compassion, and kindness towards ourselves and others. By directing positive intentions and well-wishes towards ourselves and others, we can cultivate a sense of connection and inner peace.

The Connection Between Mindfulness and Happiness

There is a strong connection between mindfulness and happiness. Mindfulness helps us cultivate a greater sense of awareness and appreciation for the present moment, which is a key ingredient for happiness. By bringing our attention to the here and now, we can fully engage with life and find joy in the simple pleasures.

Scientific studies have shown that mindfulness can increase positive emotions such as happiness, joy, and contentment. It can also decrease negative emotions such as stress, anxiety, and depression. By practicing mindfulness, we can develop a more positive outlook on life and experience greater overall happiness.

Many individuals have found happiness through the practice of mindfulness. They have reported feeling more grateful, content, and fulfilled in their daily lives. They have experienced a greater sense of connection with themselves and others, leading to deeper relationships and a greater sense of purpose.

The Science Behind Mindfulness and Its Effects on the Brain

The practice of mindfulness has been shown to have profound effects on the brain. When we engage in mindfulness practices, certain areas of the brain associated with attention, emotion regulation, and self-awareness are activated. These areas include the prefrontal cortex, anterior cingulate cortex, and insula.

Scientific studies have shown that regular mindfulness practice can lead to structural changes in the brain, such as increased gray matter density in areas associated with attention and emotional regulation. It can also lead to functional changes in the brain, such as increased connectivity between different brain regions involved in attention and emotion regulation.

These changes in the brain can have a wide range of benefits, including improved cognitive function, increased emotional resilience, and enhanced overall well-being. A "mindful brain" is more adaptable, flexible, and resilient, allowing us to navigate life's challenges with greater ease and grace.

Mindfulness Practices to Boost Happiness

There are various mindfulness practices that can help boost happiness. One such practice is gratitude meditation, where we focus on cultivating feelings of gratitude for the people, things, and experiences in our lives. By directing our attention towards what we are grateful for, we can shift our focus from what is lacking to what is abundant, leading to greater happiness and contentment.

Mindful eating is another practice that can boost happiness. By bringing our attention to the sensory experience of eating, such as the taste, texture, and smell of food, we can cultivate a greater sense of enjoyment and satisfaction. By eating mindfully, we can also develop a healthier relationship with food and make more conscious choices about what we eat.

Mindful communication involves bringing our full presence and attention to our interactions with others. By listening deeply and speaking mindfully, we can cultivate greater understanding, empathy, and connection in our relationships. This can lead to greater happiness and fulfillment in our interactions with others.

Mindful listening is a practice that involves bringing our full attention to the person who is speaking without interrupting or judging. By truly listening to others with an open heart and mind, we can cultivate deeper connections and understanding in our relationships.

How Mindfulness Helps in Managing Stress and Anxiety

Stress and anxiety are common experiences in today's fast-paced world. They can have a significant impact on our physical, mental, and emotional well-being. Mindfulness can be a powerful tool for managing stress and anxiety.

Stress is a physiological response to a perceived threat or challenge. It triggers the release of stress hormones such as cortisol, which can have negative effects on our health and well-being. By practicing mindfulness, we can activate the body's relaxation response, which counteracts the stress response and promotes a state of calmness and relaxation.

Anxiety is a state of excessive worry or fear about future events. It can be debilitating and interfere with our daily lives. Mindfulness can help us manage anxiety by bringing our attention to the present moment and cultivating a non-judgmental attitude towards our thoughts and emotions. By observing our anxious thoughts without getting caught up in them, we can reduce their power over us and experience a greater sense of calmness and peace.

Many individuals have found relief from stress and anxiety through the practice of mindfulness. They have reported feeling more relaxed, centered, and at ease in their daily lives. They have experienced a greater sense of control over their thoughts and emotions, leading to reduced stress levels and improved overall well-being.

Mindfulness-Based Stress Reduction Techniques

Mindfulness-based stress reduction (MBSR) is a program that was developed by Jon Kabat-Zinn in the late 1970s. It combines mindfulness meditation, body awareness, and yoga to help individuals manage stress, pain, and illness. MBSR has been shown to be effective in reducing stress, anxiety, and depression, as well as improving overall well-being.

One technique used in MBSR is body scan meditation, where we systematically bring our attention to different parts of the body, starting from the top of the head down to the toes. This practice helps us develop awareness of bodily sensations and release tension or discomfort that may be present.

Mindful breathing is another technique used in MBSR. It involves bringing our attention to the sensations of the breath entering and leaving our body. By focusing on the breath, we can anchor ourselves in the present moment and cultivate a sense of calmness and relaxation.

Mindful movement, such as yoga or tai chi, is another technique used in MBSR. By bringing our attention to the sensations of movement in the body, we can cultivate a greater sense of embodiment and presence. Mindful movement can help reduce stress, improve flexibility and strength, and promote overall well-being.

Mindful eating is also a key component of MBSR. By bringing our full attention to the sensory experience of eating, we can cultivate a greater sense of enjoyment and satisfaction. Mindful eating can also help us develop a healthier relationship with food and make more conscious choices about what we eat.

Mindfulness and Its Role in Improving Relationships

Mindfulness can play a significant role in improving relationships. By bringing our full presence and attention to our interactions with others, we can cultivate deeper connections, understanding, and empathy. Mindfulness helps us become better listeners, communicators, and partners in our relationships.

When we practice mindfulness in our relationships, we are able to truly listen to others without judgment or interruption. We are able to be fully present with them, giving them our undivided attention and creating a safe space for them to express themselves. This deep listening can foster greater understanding and empathy, leading to stronger and more fulfilling relationships.

Mindfulness also helps us become more aware of our own thoughts, emotions, and reactions in our relationships. By observing our own patterns of behavior without judgment, we can become more conscious of how we may be contributing to conflicts or misunderstandings. This self-awareness allows us to take responsibility for our actions and make conscious choices about how we want to show up in our relationships.

Many individuals have experienced significant improvements in their relationships through the practice of mindfulness. They have reported feeling more connected, understood, and supported by their partners, friends, and family members. By cultivating mindfulness in their relationships, they have been able to create deeper bonds and experience greater love and fulfillment.

Incorporating Mindfulness into Your Daily Life: Tips and Tricks

Incorporating mindfulness into your daily life doesn't have to be complicated or time-consuming. There are simple ways to bring mindfulness into your everyday activities and make it a part of your routine.

One way to incorporate mindfulness into your daily life is to start your day with a few minutes of mindful breathing or meditation. Set aside a few minutes in the morning to sit quietly and bring your attention to the sensations of the breath entering and leaving your body. This can help you start your day with a sense of calmness and presence.

Another way to incorporate mindfulness into your daily life is to practice mindful eating. Take the time to savor each bite of food, noticing the flavors, textures, and smells. Eat slowly and mindfully, paying attention to the sensations in your body and the experience of nourishing yourself.

You can also practice mindfulness while doing everyday activities such as walking, showering, or brushing your teeth. Bring your full attention to the sensations of each step, the feeling of water on your skin, or the movements of your hand. By fully engaging with these activities, you can cultivate a greater sense of presence and awareness.

There are also many mindfulness apps and resources available that can support your practice. Apps such as Headspace, Calm, and Insight

Timer offer guided meditations, breathing exercises, and other mindfulness practices that you can access anytime, anywhere. These resources can help you stay consistent with your practice and provide guidance and support along the way.

Personal tips and tricks for practicing mindfulness may vary from person to person. Some individuals find it helpful to set reminders throughout the day to bring their attention back to the present moment. Others find it helpful to create a dedicated space for their mindfulness practice, such as a quiet corner in their home or office. Experiment with different techniques and find what works best for you.

In conclusion, mindfulness is a powerful practice that can help us find inner peace, happiness, and well-being in today's fast-paced world. By bringing our attention to the present moment and cultivating a non-judgmental attitude towards our thoughts and emotions, we can experience a greater sense of calmness, clarity, and connection.

The benefits of practicing mindfulness are numerous, including physical, mental, and emotional well-being. Mindfulness can help us manage stress and anxiety, improve our relationships, and enhance our overall quality of life. By incorporating mindfulness into our daily lives, we can cultivate a greater sense of presence, awareness, and gratitude.

I encourage you to start practicing mindfulness today. Start with just a few minutes each day and gradually increase the duration as you become more comfortable. Be patient with yourself and remember that mindfulness is a lifelong journey. With consistent practice and an open heart, you can experience the profound benefits of mindfulness and find peace and happiness in every moment.

Chapter 24: The Importance of Boundaries in Maintaining Healthy Relationships

Boundaries play a crucial role in maintaining healthy and fulfilling relationships. They are the invisible lines that define where one person ends and another begins, and they help to establish a sense of safety, respect, and autonomy within a relationship. Without clear boundaries, relationships can become chaotic, overwhelming, and even toxic. In this article, we will explore the importance of boundaries in relationships, how they can help maintain healthy dynamics, and how to set and communicate boundaries effectively.

What are Boundaries and Why are They Important?

Boundaries can be defined as the limits we set for ourselves and others in order to protect our physical, emotional, and mental well-being. They are the guidelines that determine what is acceptable and what is not in our relationships. Boundaries are important because they help to establish a sense of personal identity and autonomy within a relationship. They allow us to express our needs, desires, and values while also respecting the needs and boundaries of others.

Boundaries are essential in relationships because they create a sense of safety and trust. When both partners have clear boundaries, they can feel secure in expressing their thoughts, feelings, and desires without fear of judgment or rejection. Boundaries also help to prevent misunderstandings and conflicts by establishing clear expectations and guidelines for behavior.

The Role of Boundaries in Maintaining Healthy

Relationships

Boundaries play a crucial role in maintaining healthy relationships by promoting open communication, respect, and trust. When both partners have clear boundaries, they can communicate their needs and expectations openly and honestly. This allows for a deeper understanding of each other's wants and needs, which can lead to greater intimacy and connection.

Boundaries also help to prevent conflicts and misunderstandings by establishing clear guidelines for behavior. When both partners know what is acceptable and what is not, they are less likely to engage in behaviors that may hurt or disrespect the other person. This creates a sense of safety and trust within the relationship, as both partners can rely on each other to respect their boundaries.

How Lack of Boundaries Can Affect Relationships

On the other hand, a lack of boundaries can have a negative impact on relationships. Without clear boundaries, partners may become enmeshed or codependent, losing their sense of individuality and autonomy. This can lead to resentment, frustration, and a loss of personal identity within the relationship.

Lack of boundaries can also lead to conflicts and misunderstandings. When partners do not have clear guidelines for behavior, they may engage in behaviors that hurt or disrespect the other person without even realizing it. This can create a cycle of hurt and resentment, damaging the trust and intimacy within the relationship.

Setting and Communicating Boundaries in Relationships

Setting and communicating boundaries is essential for maintaining healthy relationships. Here are some steps to help you set and communicate boundaries effectively:

1. Reflect on your needs: Take some time to reflect on your own needs, desires, and values. What is important to you in a relationship? What are your deal-breakers? Understanding your own needs will help you establish clear boundaries.

2. Communicate openly: Once you have identified your boundaries, communicate them openly and honestly with your partner. Be clear about what is acceptable and what is not, and explain why these boundaries are important to you.

3. Listen to your partner: Give your partner the opportunity to express their own needs and boundaries as well. Listen actively and try to understand their perspective. This will help you establish mutual understanding and respect.

4. Be flexible: Remember that boundaries are not set in stone. They may evolve over time as the relationship grows and changes. Be open to revisiting and adjusting your boundaries as needed.

Common Types of Boundaries in Relationships

Boundaries can vary depending on the type of relationship and the individuals involved. Here are some common types of boundaries in relationships:

1. Physical boundaries: These boundaries define the level of physical contact that is acceptable within the relationship. They can include personal space, sexual boundaries, and boundaries around physical touch.

2. Emotional boundaries: Emotional boundaries define how much emotional intimacy and vulnerability is comfortable for each partner.

They involve setting limits on sharing personal information, expressing emotions, and providing emotional support.

3. Time boundaries: Time boundaries involve setting limits on how much time is spent together as a couple and how much time is spent on individual activities or with other people. They help to maintain a healthy balance between togetherness and individuality.

4. Financial boundaries: Financial boundaries involve setting limits on how money is shared and spent within the relationship. They help to establish financial independence and prevent conflicts over money.

The Benefits of Having Healthy Boundaries in Relationships

Having healthy boundaries in relationships has numerous benefits. Here are some of the key benefits:

1. Better communication: Healthy boundaries promote open and honest communication, allowing partners to express their needs, desires, and concerns without fear of judgment or rejection.

2. Increased trust: When both partners have clear boundaries, they can trust that their needs and boundaries will be respected. This creates a sense of safety and trust within the relationship.

3. Respectful conflict resolution: Boundaries help to prevent conflicts by establishing clear guidelines for behavior. When conflicts do arise, partners with healthy boundaries are more likely to address them in a respectful and constructive manner.

4. Greater intimacy: Healthy boundaries allow for deeper emotional intimacy and connection within the relationship. When both partners feel safe to express their true selves, they can develop a deeper understanding and appreciation for each other.

How to Identify and Address Boundary Violations in Relationships

It is important to be able to identify and address boundary violations in relationships in a timely and respectful manner. Here are some steps to help you address boundary violations effectively:

1. Identify the violation: Pay attention to any behaviors or actions that make you feel uncomfortable, disrespected, or violated. Trust your instincts and acknowledge when a boundary has been crossed.

2. Communicate assertively: Express your feelings and concerns assertively and directly to your partner. Use "I" statements to express how their behavior made you feel and explain why it violated your boundaries.

3. Set consequences: Clearly communicate the consequences of crossing your boundaries. This can include taking a break from the relationship, seeking therapy, or establishing new boundaries.

4. Seek support if needed: If your partner continues to violate your boundaries despite your efforts to address the issue, it may be helpful to seek support from a therapist or counselor who can help you navigate the situation.

Overcoming Challenges in Maintaining Boundaries in Relationships

Maintaining boundaries in relationships can be challenging, but it is not impossible. Here are some common challenges and strategies for overcoming them:

1. Fear of conflict: Many people avoid setting boundaries because they fear conflict or rejection. It is important to remember that setting boundaries is an act of self-care and self-respect. Practice assertiveness and remind yourself that your needs are valid.

2. Guilt and people-pleasing tendencies: People with a tendency to please others may struggle with setting and maintaining boundaries. It

is important to prioritize your own needs and remember that saying no does not make you a bad person.

3. Lack of self-awareness: Some individuals may struggle with setting boundaries because they are not fully aware of their own needs and desires. Take time for self-reflection and explore what is truly important to you in a relationship.

4. Lack of support: It can be challenging to maintain boundaries if your partner or others in your life do not respect or understand them. Seek support from friends, family, or a therapist who can help you navigate these challenges.

The Connection between Self-Care and Healthy Boundaries in Relationships

Self-care and healthy boundaries go hand in hand. Setting and maintaining boundaries is an act of self-care, as it allows you to prioritize your own needs, desires, and well-being within a relationship. When you have clear boundaries, you are better able to take care of yourself and maintain a healthy sense of self.

Self-care also helps to maintain healthy boundaries by ensuring that you have the time, energy, and resources to devote to your own needs. When you prioritize self-care, you are better able to communicate your boundaries effectively and assertively.

The Significance of Boundaries in Building Strong and Healthy Relationships

In conclusion, boundaries are essential for building strong and healthy relationships. They promote open communication, respect, and trust, while also preventing conflicts and misunderstandings. By setting and maintaining clear boundaries, individuals can establish a sense of safety, autonomy, and personal identity within their relationships.

It is important to prioritize setting and maintaining healthy boundaries in all types of relationships, whether it be romantic partnerships, friendships, or family relationships. By doing so, individuals can create a foundation of trust, respect, and mutual understanding that will contribute to the growth and longevity of their relationships. So take the time to reflect on your own needs and values, communicate them openly with your partner or loved ones, and remember that setting boundaries is an act of self-care and self-respect.

Chapter 25: From Passive to Powerful: The Benefits of Assertiveness Training

Assertiveness is a crucial skill that can greatly impact our lives and relationships. It is the ability to express our thoughts, feelings, and needs in a direct and respectful manner, while also respecting the rights and boundaries of others. Unlike aggression, which involves forcing our opinions on others, or passivity, which involves suppressing our own needs and desires, assertiveness strikes a balance between the two.

Assertiveness is important because it allows us to communicate effectively, set boundaries, resolve conflicts, and build healthy relationships. It helps us express ourselves authentically and assert our rights without infringing on the rights of others. By being assertive, we can improve our self-esteem, gain respect from others, and create a more fulfilling and satisfying life.

Defining Assertiveness: What It Is and What It Isn't

Assertiveness is often misunderstood and confused with aggression or passivity. However, there are distinct differences between these three behaviors. Assertiveness involves expressing ourselves honestly and directly, while also considering the feelings and needs of others. It is about standing up for ourselves without being disrespectful or aggressive.

Examples of assertive behavior include expressing our opinions and preferences, saying no when we don't want to do something, asking for what we need or want, and setting boundaries with others. It involves using "I" statements to express our feelings and needs, rather than blaming or attacking others.

On the other hand, aggression involves forcing our opinions on others, being disrespectful or hostile towards others, and violating their boundaries. Passivity involves suppressing our own needs and desires, avoiding conflict at all costs, and allowing others to take advantage of us.

The Benefits of Assertiveness: How It Can Improve Your Life

Assertiveness has numerous benefits that can greatly improve our lives. Firstly, it enhances our relationships by promoting open and honest communication. When we are assertive, we are able to express our thoughts and feelings clearly, which helps others understand us better. This leads to healthier and more fulfilling relationships, as there is less room for misunderstandings and resentment.

Assertiveness also improves our self-esteem and overall well-being. When we are able to assert our needs and desires, we feel more empowered and in control of our lives. This boosts our self-confidence and allows us to make choices that align with our values and goals. Additionally, assertiveness helps us avoid feelings of resentment or regret that can arise from not speaking up for ourselves.

Research has shown that assertiveness is linked to better mental health outcomes. A study published in the Journal of Counseling Psychology found that individuals who were more assertive reported lower levels of anxiety and depression. Another study published in the Journal of Personality and Social Psychology found that assertiveness was positively correlated with life satisfaction and overall well-being.

Building Confidence: The Role of Assertiveness in Self-Esteem

Assertiveness plays a crucial role in building confidence and self-esteem. When we are able to assert ourselves and express our needs, we feel more in control of our lives. This sense of control boosts our self-confidence and allows us to take risks and pursue our goals.

Assertiveness also helps us develop a positive self-image. When we are able to stand up for ourselves and assert our rights, we send a message to ourselves that we are worthy of respect. This reinforces positive beliefs about ourselves and strengthens our self-esteem.

To develop assertive behavior, it is important to practice self-awareness and identify our own needs and desires. We can then communicate these needs clearly and directly, using "I" statements to express how we feel. It is also important to practice active listening and empathy towards others, as this helps build stronger relationships based on mutual respect.

Communication Skills: How Assertiveness Can Improve Your Relationships

Assertiveness is a key component of effective communication. When we are assertive, we are able to express ourselves clearly and honestly, while also listening to and respecting the perspectives of others. This leads to better understanding and stronger relationships.

Assertiveness improves communication by reducing misunderstandings and conflicts. When we are able to express our thoughts and feelings clearly, others are more likely to understand us and respond in a positive manner. This reduces the chances of miscommunication or resentment building up over time.

To communicate assertively, it is important to use clear and direct language. We should express our thoughts and feelings using "I" statements, rather than blaming or attacking others. It is also important to listen actively and empathetically, allowing others to express themselves without interruption or judgment.

Setting Boundaries: The Importance of Saying "No"

Setting boundaries is an essential part of assertiveness. It involves knowing our limits and communicating them to others in a respectful manner. By setting boundaries, we protect our own well-being and ensure that our needs are met.

Saying "no" is an important aspect of setting boundaries. It allows us to prioritize our own needs and avoid taking on more than we can handle. When we say "no" assertively, we are able to communicate our limits without feeling guilty or obligated.

To set boundaries assertively, it is important to be clear and direct in our communication. We should express our needs and limits using "I" statements, while also being respectful of the other person's feelings. It is also important to be consistent in enforcing our boundaries and not allowing others to cross them.

Conflict Resolution: Using Assertiveness to Resolve Disagreements

Assertiveness is a valuable tool for resolving conflicts and disagreements. When we are assertive, we are able to express our concerns and needs in a respectful manner, while also listening to the perspectives of others. This promotes open and honest communication, which is essential for finding mutually beneficial solutions.

Assertive conflict resolution involves expressing our concerns and needs clearly and directly, without attacking or blaming others. We should use "I" statements to express how we feel and what we need, while also being open to hearing the other person's perspective. It is important to focus on finding a solution that meets the needs of both parties, rather than trying to win the argument.

By using assertiveness in conflict resolution, we can avoid escalating the situation into aggression or passivity. We can find common ground and work towards a resolution that is fair and respectful to all parties involved.

Overcoming Fear: How Assertiveness Can Help You Face Your Fears

Assertiveness is a powerful tool for overcoming fear and anxiety. When we are able to assert ourselves and express our needs, we gain a sense of control over our lives. This control helps us face our fears and take action towards overcoming them.

By being assertive, we can challenge our negative beliefs and replace them with more positive and empowering ones. When we assert ourselves and see positive outcomes, we build confidence in our ability to face our fears. This confidence allows us to take small steps towards overcoming our fears, gradually expanding our comfort zone.

To use assertiveness to face fears, it is important to identify the specific fears that are holding us back. We can then practice assertive behavior in situations that trigger these fears, gradually building up our confidence. It is also helpful to seek support from others who can provide encouragement and guidance along the way.

Assertiveness in the Workplace: Advantages for Career Advancement

Assertiveness is highly valued in the workplace and can greatly contribute to career advancement. When we are able to assert ourselves and communicate effectively, we are more likely to be seen as confident and capable by our colleagues and superiors.

Assertiveness in the workplace involves expressing our ideas and opinions clearly and confidently, while also listening to and respecting the perspectives of others. It also involves advocating for ourselves and our needs, such as asking for a raise or promotion.

By being assertive in the workplace, we can gain respect from others and create opportunities for career advancement. We are more likely to be given challenging assignments, be considered for leadership roles, and have our ideas taken seriously. Assertiveness also helps us navigate workplace conflicts and negotiate effectively.

Assertiveness Training Techniques: Tips for Developing Assertive Behavior

Developing assertive behavior requires practice and self-awareness. Here are some tips for developing assertiveness:

1. Identify your needs and desires: Take the time to reflect on your own needs and desires. What are your values and goals? What do you need in order to feel fulfilled and satisfied?

2. Practice self-expression: Start by expressing your thoughts and feelings in low-stakes situations. Practice using "I" statements to express how you feel and what you need.

3. Use assertive body language: Stand tall, make eye contact, and speak clearly when expressing yourself. Use confident body language to reinforce your assertiveness.

4. Practice active listening: When others are speaking, listen actively and empathetically. Show that you value their perspective by nodding, maintaining eye contact, and asking clarifying questions.

5. Set boundaries: Practice saying "no" when you don't want to do something or when it goes against your values or limits. Be clear and direct in your communication.

6. Seek support: Surround yourself with supportive individuals who encourage your assertiveness. Seek out assertiveness training programs or workshops that can provide guidance and practice opportunities.

Embracing Your Power Through Assertiveness

Assertiveness is a powerful skill that can greatly impact our lives and relationships. By embracing our power through assertiveness, we can improve our communication, build confidence, set boundaries, resolve conflicts, overcome fear, advance in our careers, and create a more fulfilling and satisfying life.

It is important to remember that assertiveness is not about being aggressive or forcing our opinions on others. It is about expressing ourselves honestly and respectfully, while also considering the feelings and needs of others. By practicing assertiveness, we can find a balance between our own needs and the needs of others, creating healthier and more fulfilling relationships.

So, embrace your power through assertiveness and start living a more authentic and empowered life. Practice expressing yourself honestly and respectfully, set boundaries that protect your well-being, and resolve conflicts in a fair and respectful manner. By doing so, you will reap the numerous benefits of assertiveness and create a life that aligns with your values and goals.

Chapter 26: Mastering Your Money: Essential Financial Management Tips for 27-Year-Olds

Financial planning is a crucial aspect of life, especially when you reach the age of 27. At this stage, you have likely completed your education, started your career, and are beginning to establish yourself financially. It is essential to have a solid financial plan in place to ensure that you are making the most of your money and setting yourself up for a secure future.

Setting Financial Goals: Why It Matters at 27

Setting financial goals at the age of 27 is crucial because it allows you to have a clear direction and purpose for your money. By setting goals, you can prioritize your spending and saving habits, making sure that you are working towards achieving what is most important to you.

Some examples of financial goals to set at 27 include saving for a down payment on a house, paying off student loans, starting an investment portfolio, or building an emergency fund. These goals will vary depending on your individual circumstances and aspirations. The key is to set goals that are specific, measurable, achievable, relevant, and time-bound (SMART).

Budgeting 101: How to Create and Stick to a Budget

Creating and sticking to a budget is an essential skill for financial success at any age, but it becomes even more critical at 27 when you have more financial responsibilities. A budget helps you track your income and expenses, ensuring that you are living within your means and saving for your goals.

To create a budget, start by listing all of your sources of income and then subtracting your fixed expenses such as rent/mortgage, utilities, transportation costs, and debt payments. Next, allocate funds for variable expenses such as groceries, entertainment, and dining out. Finally, determine how much you want to save each month towards your financial goals.

Sticking to a budget requires discipline and self-control. It can be helpful to automate savings by setting up automatic transfers from your checking account to your savings account. Additionally, track your spending regularly and make adjustments as needed to stay on track.

The Importance of Saving: Tips for Building Your Emergency Fund

Building an emergency fund is a crucial aspect of financial planning at 27. An emergency fund is a savings account that is specifically designated for unexpected expenses such as medical bills, car repairs, or job loss. Having an emergency fund provides a financial safety net and helps prevent you from going into debt when unexpected expenses arise.

To build an emergency fund, start by setting a savings goal. Aim to save three to six months' worth of living expenses. This amount will vary depending on your individual circumstances and comfort level. Next, create a separate savings account specifically for your emergency fund. Set up automatic transfers from your checking account to this savings account each month.

It can be challenging to save for emergencies when you have other financial goals, but it is essential to prioritize building your emergency fund. Consider cutting back on discretionary expenses or finding ways to increase your income to accelerate your savings.

Managing Debt: Strategies for Paying Off Student

Loans and Credit Card Debt

Debt can be a significant burden on your finances, especially at 27 when you may still be paying off student loans or have accumulated credit card debt. It is crucial to have a strategy in place for paying off debt and managing it effectively.

Start by understanding the different types of debt you have and their impact on your finances. Student loans typically have lower interest rates and longer repayment terms, making them more manageable. Credit card debt, on the other hand, often carries high-interest rates, making it more challenging to pay off.

To pay off student loans, consider making extra payments towards the principal balance each month or refinancing to get a lower interest rate. For credit card debt, focus on paying off the highest interest rate balances first while making minimum payments on the rest.

It can be helpful to create a debt repayment plan and track your progress. Consider using the debt snowball or debt avalanche method to pay off debt systematically. The key is to stay committed and avoid accumulating more debt while you are paying off existing balances.

Investing for the Future: How to Start Building Your Retirement Savings

While retirement may seem far away at 27, it is never too early to start saving for it. In fact, starting early gives you a significant advantage due to the power of compound interest. Compound interest allows your money to grow exponentially over time, so the earlier you start investing, the more time your money has to grow.

To start building your retirement savings, consider opening an individual retirement account (IRA) or contributing to your employer's 401(k) plan if available. Take advantage of any employer matching contributions as this is essentially free money.

When investing for retirement, it is essential to diversify your portfolio and take a long-term approach. Consider investing in a mix of stocks, bonds, and other assets that align with your risk tolerance and financial goals. Regularly review and rebalance your portfolio as needed.

Understanding Credit Scores: How to Improve Your Credit and Keep It Healthy

Your credit score plays a significant role in your financial life, impacting your ability to get approved for loans, rent an apartment, or even secure a job. It is crucial to understand the basics of credit scores and take steps to improve and maintain a healthy credit score.

Your credit score is a three-digit number that represents your creditworthiness based on factors such as payment history, credit utilization, length of credit history, types of credit used, and new credit inquiries. A higher credit score indicates lower risk to lenders.

To improve your credit score, focus on making all of your payments on time, keeping your credit utilization ratio below 30%, and avoiding opening too many new accounts at once. Regularly check your credit report for errors and dispute any inaccuracies.

Maintaining a healthy credit score requires responsible credit management. Avoid maxing out your credit cards, keep old accounts open to maintain a long credit history, and only apply for new credit when necessary.

Tax Planning: What You Need to Know About Filing Your Taxes at 27

Filing taxes can be overwhelming, but it is an essential part of financial planning at 27. Understanding the basics of tax filing and planning can help you maximize your deductions and minimize your tax liability.

Start by familiarizing yourself with the different types of income and deductions you may have. This can include income from your job, investments, or side hustles, as well as deductions for student loan interest, mortgage interest, or charitable contributions.

Consider using tax software or working with a tax professional to ensure that you are filing your taxes correctly and taking advantage of all available deductions and credits. Keep organized records of your income and expenses throughout the year to make tax filing easier.

Additionally, consider adjusting your tax withholding if necessary to avoid owing a large amount or receiving a significant refund. Use the IRS withholding calculator to determine the appropriate amount to withhold from your paycheck.

Building a Strong Financial Foundation: Tips for Creating a Financial Plan

Creating a financial plan is essential for building a strong financial foundation at 27. A financial plan outlines your goals, strategies, and action steps for achieving financial success.

Start by assessing your current financial situation, including your income, expenses, assets, and liabilities. Next, identify your short-term and long-term financial goals. These can include saving for a down payment on a house, paying off debt, starting a business, or retiring early.

Once you have identified your goals, create a plan for achieving them. This may include creating a budget, setting up automatic savings contributions, paying off debt systematically, and investing for the future. Regularly review and adjust your financial plan as needed to stay on track.

Consider working with a financial advisor to help you create a comprehensive financial plan that aligns with your goals and risk tolerance. A financial advisor can provide guidance and expertise to help you make informed financial decisions.

The Power of Compound Interest: How to Make Your Money Work for You

Compound interest is a powerful tool for building wealth, and understanding how it works can help you make your money work for you. Compound interest allows your money to grow exponentially over time, as the interest earned is reinvested and earns additional interest.

To take advantage of compound interest, start by saving and investing early. The earlier you start, the more time your money has to grow. Consider opening an investment account and regularly contribute to it.

When investing, focus on long-term growth and diversification. Consider investing in a mix of stocks, bonds, and other assets that align with your risk tolerance and financial goals. Regularly review and rebalance your portfolio as needed.

Avoid withdrawing from your investments prematurely, as this can hinder the power of compound interest. Instead, let your investments grow over time and reinvest any dividends or interest earned.

Protecting Your Assets: Essential Insurance Policies for 27-Year-Olds

Insurance is an essential aspect of financial planning at 27. It helps protect your assets and provides financial security in the event of unexpected events such as accidents, illnesses, or natural disasters.

Some essential insurance policies for 27-year-olds include health insurance, renter's or homeowner's insurance, auto insurance, and disability insurance. Health insurance provides coverage for medical expenses, while renter's or homeowner's insurance protects your belongings and provides liability coverage. Auto insurance is required if you own a vehicle, and disability insurance provides income replacement if you are unable to work due to illness or injury.

Consider working with an insurance agent to assess your insurance needs and find the best policies for your situation. Regularly review your insurance coverage and make adjustments as needed to ensure that you are adequately protected.

Avoiding Common Financial Mistakes: Tips for Making Smart Money Choices at 27

At 27, it is crucial to avoid common financial mistakes that can hinder your financial progress. By making smart money choices, you can set yourself up for long-term success.

One common mistake is overspending and living beyond your means. It is essential to create a budget and stick to it, prioritizing your spending and saving habits. Avoid accumulating unnecessary debt and focus on building an emergency fund and saving for your goals.

Another mistake is not taking advantage of employer benefits such as retirement plans or health insurance. Make sure to understand and utilize all of the benefits available to you through your employer.

Additionally, avoid making impulsive financial decisions without considering the long-term consequences. Take the time to research and evaluate your options before making any major financial decisions.

Financial planning at 27 is crucial for setting yourself up for a secure future. By setting financial goals, creating a budget, saving, managing debt, investing, understanding credit scores, tax planning, creating a financial plan, taking advantage of compound interest, protecting your assets with insurance, and avoiding common financial mistakes, you can build a strong financial foundation.

Take action today and start planning your finances. The earlier you start, the more time you have to achieve your goals and build wealth. Seek guidance from professionals if needed and stay committed to your financial plan. With discipline and perseverance, you can achieve financial success at 27 and beyond.

Chapter 27: Eating for Energy: How Proper Nutrition Can Boost Your Workout

Proper nutrition plays a crucial role in athletic performance. Whether you're a professional athlete or a recreational fitness enthusiast, what you eat can significantly impact your energy levels, endurance, strength, and overall performance. Fueling your body with the right nutrients is essential for optimal performance and recovery. In this article, we will explore the importance of macronutrients such as carbohydrates, proteins, and fats, as well as the role of hydration and timing of meals and snacks in maximizing energy and performance.

Understanding Macronutrients: Carbohydrates, Proteins, and Fats

Macronutrients are the nutrients that provide energy to the body in the form of calories. They include carbohydrates, proteins, and fats. Each macronutrient has a specific role in the body and is essential for various bodily functions.

Carbohydrates are the body's primary source of energy. They are broken down into glucose, which is used by the muscles and brain for fuel. Carbohydrates can be found in foods such as grains, fruits, vegetables, and legumes. They are especially important for endurance athletes who engage in long-duration activities such as running or cycling.

Proteins are essential for building and repairing muscle tissue. They are made up of amino acids, which are the building blocks of protein. Athletes require more protein than sedentary individuals to support muscle growth and repair. Good sources of protein include lean meats, poultry, fish, eggs, dairy products, legumes, and tofu.

Fats are another important macronutrient that provides energy to the body. They are necessary for hormone production, insulation of organs, and absorption of fat-soluble vitamins. Healthy fats can be found in foods such as avocados, nuts, seeds, olive oil, and fatty fish like salmon.

The Role of Carbohydrates in Providing Energy for Workouts

Carbohydrates are the body's preferred source of energy during exercise. When you consume carbohydrates, they are broken down into glucose, which is stored in the muscles and liver as glycogen. During exercise, the body taps into these glycogen stores to provide energy.

Carbohydrates are especially important for endurance athletes who engage in long-duration activities. Studies have shown that consuming carbohydrates during prolonged exercise can delay fatigue and improve performance. Carbohydrate-rich foods such as pasta, rice, bread, and fruits should be included in the diet of athletes who engage in endurance activities.

For high-intensity workouts, carbohydrates are also crucial. The body relies on glycogen stores for quick bursts of energy during intense exercise. Consuming carbohydrates before a high-intensity workout can help ensure that your glycogen stores are adequately replenished, allowing you to perform at your best.

Protein: Essential for Building and Repairing Muscle Tissue

Protein is essential for athletes and active individuals as it plays a crucial role in building and repairing muscle tissue. During exercise, muscle fibers break down, and protein is needed to repair and rebuild these fibers, leading to muscle growth and strength gains.

Consuming an adequate amount of protein is especially important for strength athletes and those looking to build muscle mass. Research has shown that consuming protein immediately after resistance exercise can enhance muscle protein synthesis, leading to greater gains in muscle mass and strength.

Good sources of protein include lean meats, poultry, fish, eggs, dairy products, legumes, and tofu. It's important to spread your protein intake throughout the day to ensure that your muscles have a constant supply of amino acids for repair and growth.

The Benefits of Healthy Fats for Endurance and Stamina

While carbohydrates are the body's primary source of energy during exercise, healthy fats also play a role in improving endurance and stamina. Fats are a concentrated source of energy and can provide a steady supply of fuel during long-duration activities.

In addition to providing energy, healthy fats are also important for hormone production and absorption of fat-soluble vitamins. Including sources of healthy fats such as avocados, nuts, seeds, and olive oil in your diet can help improve endurance and stamina during exercise.

Hydration: The Key to Maintaining Energy Levels During Exercise

Proper hydration is essential for athletic performance. Dehydration can negatively impact energy levels, endurance, and overall performance. When you exercise, you lose water through sweat, and if this water is not replaced, it can lead to dehydration.

Dehydration can cause fatigue, muscle cramps, dizziness, and decreased cognitive function. To stay properly hydrated, it's important to drink fluids before, during, and after exercise. Water is usually sufficient for most workouts, but for intense or prolonged exercise, sports drinks that contain electrolytes may be beneficial.

Pre-Workout Nutrition: What to Eat and When to Eat It

Fueling your body with the right nutrients before a workout is essential for optimal performance. The timing and composition of your pre-workout meal or snack can impact your energy levels and endurance.

Ideally, you should consume a meal or snack that contains a combination of carbohydrates and protein about 1-3 hours before your workout. This will provide your body with the necessary fuel to perform at its best. Good pre-workout food choices include whole grains, fruits, lean proteins, and healthy fats.

If you're short on time or prefer not to eat a full meal before a workout, a small snack that contains carbohydrates and protein can also be beneficial. Examples of pre-workout snacks include a banana with peanut butter, Greek yogurt with berries, or a protein shake.

Post-Workout Nutrition: Why It Matters for Recovery and Growth

Post-workout nutrition is just as important as pre-workout nutrition. After exercise, your body needs to replenish glycogen stores, repair muscle tissue, and promote recovery. Consuming the right nutrients after a workout can help facilitate these processes.

Protein is particularly important after a workout as it helps repair and rebuild muscle tissue. Consuming a combination of carbohydrates and protein within 30-60 minutes after exercise can enhance muscle protein synthesis and glycogen replenishment.

Good post-workout food choices include lean meats, poultry, fish, eggs, dairy products, legumes, and tofu for protein, and carbohydrates such as fruits, whole grains, and potatoes for glycogen replenishment. Including some healthy fats in your post-workout meal or snack can also be beneficial for overall recovery.

The Importance of Timing Your Meals and Snacks for Optimal Energy

In addition to the composition of your meals and snacks, the timing of your nutrition can also impact your energy levels and performance. Eating too close to a workout can cause digestive discomfort, while eating too far in advance may leave you feeling hungry and low on energy.

As a general guideline, it's best to eat a full meal containing carbohydrates and protein about 2-3 hours before a workout. This will give your body enough time to digest the food and provide you with sustained energy throughout your workout.

If you're eating a smaller snack before a workout, aim to consume it about 30-60 minutes before exercise. This will give your body enough time to digest the food without causing any discomfort during your workout.

Choosing the Right Foods for Your Fitness Goals and Dietary Needs

When it comes to choosing the right foods for your fitness goals and dietary needs, it's important to consider factors such as calorie intake, macronutrient distribution, and individual preferences.

If your goal is to lose weight or reduce body fat, you may need to create a calorie deficit by consuming fewer calories than you burn. In this case, it's important to choose nutrient-dense foods that are low in calories but high in vitamins, minerals, and fiber.

If your goal is to build muscle or improve athletic performance, you may need to consume more calories and increase your protein intake.

Including a variety of nutrient-dense foods such as lean meats, poultry, fish, fruits, vegetables, whole grains, and healthy fats can help support your fitness goals.

It's also important to consider any dietary restrictions or preferences you may have. If you follow a vegetarian or vegan diet, for example, you'll need to ensure that you're getting enough protein from plant-based sources such as legumes, tofu, tempeh, and seitan.

Combining Proper Nutrition with Exercise for Maximum Energy and Performance

Proper nutrition and exercise go hand in hand when it comes to maximizing energy and performance. While exercise is crucial for building strength and endurance, without the right fuel, your body won't be able to perform at its best.

By fueling your body with the right nutrients before and after exercise, you can optimize energy levels, enhance performance, and promote recovery. It's important to find the right balance between nutrition and exercise to support your fitness goals and overall well-being.

Proper nutrition is essential for athletic performance. By understanding the role of macronutrients such as carbohydrates, proteins, and fats, as well as the importance of hydration and timing of meals and snacks, you can maximize your energy levels and performance.

Fueling your body with the right nutrients before a workout can provide you with sustained energy and endurance. Consuming the right nutrients after a workout can promote recovery and muscle growth. By choosing the right foods for your fitness goals and dietary needs, you can support your overall health and well-being.

Make nutrition a priority in your fitness journey and see how it can positively impact your energy levels, performance, and overall results. Remember, it's not just about what you do in the gym or on the field, but also what you put into your body that can make a significant difference.

Chapter 29: Speak Up and Stand Out: Developing Your Advocacy Voice

Advocacy voice is the power to speak up and take action on issues that matter to you. It is the ability to use your voice to influence change, raise awareness, and make a difference in the world. Advocacy voice is crucial because it allows individuals to address social, political, and environmental issues that impact their lives and the lives of others.

Advocacy voice has made a significant impact in various contexts throughout history. For example, the civil rights movement in the United States was fueled by the advocacy voice of individuals like Martin Luther King Jr., who spoke out against racial injustice and fought for equality. Their advocacy voice led to significant legislative changes and a shift in societal attitudes.

In the environmental movement, advocacy voice has played a crucial role in raising awareness about climate change and pushing for sustainable practices. Organizations like Greenpeace and individuals like Greta Thunberg have used their advocacy voice to mobilize millions of people around the world and put pressure on governments and corporations to take action.

Understanding Your Personal Advocacy Style

Everyone has their own unique advocacy style, which is influenced by their personality, values, and experiences. It is essential to identify your personal advocacy style so that you can leverage your strengths and work on areas for improvement.

Some people may have an assertive advocacy style, where they are comfortable speaking up and taking charge in advocating for their cause. Others may have a more collaborative style, preferring to work with others and build partnerships to achieve their goals.

Understanding your personal advocacy style will help you determine the most effective strategies for making an impact.

To identify your advocacy style, reflect on your past experiences of advocating for something you believe in. Think about how you approached the situation, what strategies you used, and how successful you were. Consider your strengths and weaknesses as an advocate, such as your communication skills, ability to build relationships, or knowledge of the issue. This self-reflection will give you valuable insights into your personal advocacy style.

Identifying Your Advocacy Goals and Objectives

Setting clear goals and objectives is crucial for effective advocacy. Without a clear direction, it can be challenging to make progress and measure the impact of your advocacy efforts. When identifying your advocacy goals and objectives, consider the following strategies:

1. Identify the issues that matter most to you: Start by brainstorming a list of issues that you are passionate about and want to advocate for. Consider your personal experiences, values, and the impact you want to make.

2. Research and prioritize: Once you have a list of potential issues, research each one to understand the current state of affairs, existing advocacy efforts, and potential areas for improvement. Prioritize the issues based on their urgency, feasibility, and alignment with your values.

3. Set SMART goals: SMART stands for Specific, Measurable, Achievable, Relevant, and Time-bound. Set goals that are specific and clearly defined, measurable so that you can track progress, achievable within a reasonable timeframe, relevant to your cause, and time-bound to create a sense of urgency.

By setting clear goals and objectives, you will have a roadmap for your advocacy work and be better equipped to make a meaningful impact.

Building Confidence in Your Advocacy Skills

Advocacy can be intimidating, especially if you are new to it or feel unsure about your abilities. However, building confidence in your advocacy skills is essential for effectively advocating for your cause. Here are some common challenges people face when advocating and tips for overcoming them:

1. Fear of public speaking: Many people fear public speaking, but it is a crucial skill in advocacy. To overcome this fear, practice speaking in front of others or join a public speaking group. Start with small audiences and gradually work your way up to larger ones.

2. Lack of knowledge: Feeling like you don't know enough about the issue you are advocating for can be discouraging. Take the time to educate yourself by reading books, attending workshops or webinars, and connecting with experts in the field. The more knowledge you have, the more confident you will feel.

3. Imposter syndrome: Imposter syndrome is the feeling that you are not qualified or deserving of your role as an advocate. Remember that everyone has something valuable to contribute, and your unique perspective and experiences are valuable assets. Surround yourself with a supportive network of like-minded individuals who can provide encouragement and validation.

Building confidence in your advocacy skills takes time and practice. Be patient with yourself and celebrate small victories along the way.

Developing Effective Communication Strategies

Effective communication is crucial in advocacy because it allows you to convey your message clearly and persuasively. Here are some strategies for developing effective communication strategies:

1. Know your audience: Tailor your message to the specific audience you are trying to reach. Consider their values, beliefs, and level of knowledge on the issue. Use language and examples that

resonate with them to increase the chances of your message being heard and understood.

2. Use different mediums: Different people respond to different forms of communication. Some may prefer written materials, while others may prefer videos or social media posts. Use a variety of mediums to reach a broader audience and make your message more accessible.

3. Be concise and compelling: In advocacy, attention spans are short, so it is essential to get your message across quickly and effectively. Craft a concise and compelling message that highlights the key points and captures the attention of your audience.

By developing effective communication strategies, you will be able to effectively convey your message and engage others in your cause.

The Power of Storytelling in Advocacy

Storytelling is a powerful tool in advocacy because it allows you to connect with others on an emotional level and make your message more relatable. Here are some tips for crafting and sharing compelling stories:

1. Start with a personal connection: Begin your story by sharing a personal experience or anecdote that illustrates the issue you are advocating for. This will help your audience connect with the issue on a deeper level and understand its impact.

2. Use vivid language and imagery: Paint a picture with your words to make your story come alive. Use descriptive language and vivid imagery to engage the senses and create a lasting impression.

3. Highlight the human element: Focus on the people affected by the issue you are advocating for. Share their stories, struggles, and triumphs to humanize the issue and make it more relatable.

By incorporating storytelling into your advocacy efforts, you will be able to capture the attention of your audience and inspire them to take action.

The Role of Active Listening in Advocacy

Active listening is a crucial skill in advocacy because it allows you to understand the perspectives and concerns of others, build relationships, and find common ground. Here are some strategies for practicing active listening:

1. Be fully present: When engaging in a conversation or meeting, be fully present and give your undivided attention to the person speaking. Put away distractions like phones or laptops and focus on what they are saying.

2. Ask open-ended questions: Encourage others to share their thoughts and feelings by asking open-ended questions that require more than a simple yes or no answer. This will help you gain a deeper understanding of their perspective.

3. Reflect back what you hear: After someone has finished speaking, summarize what you heard to ensure that you understood their message correctly. This shows that you were actively listening and validates their perspective.

By practicing active listening, you will be able to build stronger relationships, find common ground with others, and collaborate more effectively in your advocacy work.

Overcoming Fear and Resistance in Advocacy

Fear and resistance are common obstacles that people face when advocating for their cause. Here are some common fears and resistance people face and tips for overcoming them:

1. Fear of criticism: Many people fear being criticized or judged for their advocacy work. Remember that criticism is a natural part of the process, and not everyone will agree with you. Focus on the positive impact you are making and surround yourself with a supportive network.

2. Resistance from others: It is common to face resistance from others who may not share your views or be open to change. Stay focused on your goals and objectives, and be prepared to address concerns or objections in a respectful and constructive manner.

3. Fear of failure: Advocacy is not always easy, and setbacks are inevitable. Embrace failure as an opportunity to learn and grow, and remember that even small victories can make a significant impact.

By acknowledging and addressing your fears and resistance, you will be better equipped to stay motivated and continue advocating for your cause.

Collaborating with Others to Amplify Your Voice

Collaboration is essential in advocacy because it allows you to amplify your voice, pool resources, and achieve greater impact. Here are some strategies for building partnerships and coalitions:

1. Identify like-minded individuals and organizations: Reach out to individuals and organizations that share your values and goals. Attend networking events, join online communities, or participate in advocacy campaigns to connect with others who are passionate about similar issues.

2. Establish shared goals and objectives: When forming partnerships or coalitions, establish shared goals and objectives to ensure that everyone is working towards a common purpose. Clearly define roles and responsibilities to avoid confusion or conflicts.

3. Leverage each other's strengths: Each individual or organization brings unique strengths and resources to the table. Identify these strengths and find ways to leverage them to achieve greater impact together.

By collaborating with others, you will be able to amplify your voice, share resources, and achieve greater impact in your advocacy work.

Navigating Challenging Conversations and Situations

Challenging conversations and situations are inevitable in advocacy, but they can also be opportunities for growth and learning. Here are some tips for handling difficult conversations and situations:

1. Stay calm and composed: It is natural to feel defensive or emotional during challenging conversations, but it is essential to stay calm and composed. Take deep breaths, listen actively, and respond thoughtfully rather than reactively.

2. Seek common ground: Look for areas of agreement or shared values to find common ground with the person you are engaging with. This will help build rapport and create a more constructive dialogue.

3. Focus on the issue, not the person: Keep the conversation focused on the issue at hand rather than attacking or criticizing the person you are engaging with. This will help keep the conversation productive and respectful.

By staying calm and focused during challenging conversations and situations, you will be better equipped to navigate them effectively and achieve your advocacy goals.

Continuing to Grow and Refine Your Advocacy Voice

Advocacy is an ongoing journey of learning and growth. Here are some strategies for continuing to develop your skills and refine your message:

1. Stay informed: Stay up to date on the latest research, news, and developments related to your cause. Attend conferences, workshops, or webinars, read books or articles, and connect with experts in the field.

2. Reflect on your experiences: Regularly reflect on your advocacy experiences to identify areas for improvement and celebrate successes. Consider what worked well, what didn't, and how you can apply these lessons moving forward.

3. Seek feedback: Ask for feedback from trusted mentors, colleagues, or members of your advocacy network. Their insights can provide valuable perspectives and help you refine your message or approach.

By continuing to grow and refine your advocacy voice, you will be able to make a more significant impact and effectively advocate for your cause.

Advocacy voice is a powerful tool for creating change and making a difference in the world. By understanding your personal advocacy style, setting clear goals and objectives, building confidence in your skills, developing effective communication strategies, harnessing the power of storytelling and active listening, overcoming fear and resistance, collaborating with others, navigating challenging conversations and situations, and continuing to grow and refine your advocacy voice, you will be well-equipped to advocate for the issues that matter to you. Use your advocacy voice to make a difference and create a better world for all.

Chapter 30: From Surviving to Thriving: The Role of Hope and Resilience in Overcoming Challenges

Hope and resilience are two powerful qualities that can help individuals overcome challenges and achieve success. In the face of adversity, having hope can motivate and inspire us to keep pushing forward, while resilience allows us to bounce back from setbacks and failures. Developing a resilient mindset is crucial for navigating through life's ups and downs, and it can lead to personal growth and long-term success.

Understanding the Concept of Resilience

Resilience can be defined as the ability to adapt and bounce back from difficult situations. It is not about being tough or invincible, but rather about being able to face challenges head-on and come out stronger on the other side. Resilient individuals are able to maintain a positive outlook, persevere through setbacks, and learn from failures.

Resilience is not something that people are born with; it is a skill that can be developed over time. It involves building emotional strength, developing coping strategies, and cultivating a growth mindset. Resilient individuals are able to see setbacks as opportunities for growth and learning, rather than as insurmountable obstacles.

The Importance of Hope in Overcoming Challenges

Hope plays a crucial role in overcoming challenges because it provides us with motivation and inspiration. When we have hope, we believe that things can get better, even in the face of adversity. It gives us the strength to keep going when things get tough and helps us maintain a positive outlook.

Hope is closely linked to resilience because it allows us to bounce back from setbacks and failures. When we have hope, we are more likely to persevere through difficult times and find solutions to our problems. It gives us the confidence to take risks and try new things, even when the odds are stacked against us.

How to Cultivate Hope in Challenging Situations

Cultivating hope in challenging situations requires maintaining a positive outlook and setting realistic goals. One strategy for maintaining a positive outlook is to focus on the things that are going well in our lives, rather than dwelling on the negatives. This can be done by practicing gratitude and regularly reminding ourselves of the things we are thankful for.

Setting realistic goals is also important for cultivating hope. When we set goals that are achievable, we are more likely to believe that we can overcome challenges and achieve success. It is important to break larger goals down into smaller, manageable steps, and to celebrate each small victory along the way.

The Role of Positive Thinking in Building Resilience

Positive thinking plays a crucial role in building resilience because it helps us reframe negative thoughts and maintain a positive outlook. Positive self-talk is a powerful tool for building resilience because it allows us to challenge negative beliefs and replace them with positive affirmations.

Reframing negative thoughts involves consciously replacing negative thoughts with positive ones. For example, instead of thinking "I can't do this," we can reframe it as "I can do this if I put in the effort and stay persistent." By reframing negative thoughts, we can change our mindset and build resilience.

Developing Coping Strategies for Adversity

Developing coping strategies for adversity is an important part of building resilience. Coping strategies involve identifying and managing stressors, as well as practicing self-care. It is important to recognize when we are feeling overwhelmed or stressed and to take steps to manage these feelings.

Identifying stressors involves recognizing the things that trigger stress or anxiety in our lives. Once we have identified these stressors, we can take steps to manage them, such as practicing relaxation techniques or seeking support from others. Self-care is also crucial for building resilience because it allows us to recharge and take care of our physical and emotional well-being.

The Importance of Social Support in Building Resilience

Having a strong support system is crucial for building resilience. Social support provides us with a sense of belonging and connection, and it can help us navigate through difficult times. When we have people who believe in us and support us, we are more likely to believe in ourselves and bounce back from setbacks.

Building and maintaining social connections involves reaching out to others and nurturing relationships. This can be done by joining clubs or organizations, volunteering, or simply reaching out to friends and family members. It is important to surround ourselves with positive and supportive people who will lift us up and encourage us to keep going.

Overcoming Setbacks and Failures with

Resilience

Setbacks and failures are inevitable in life, but it is how we respond to them that determines our level of resilience. When faced with a setback or failure, it is important to take the time to process our emotions and reflect on what went wrong. This allows us to learn from our mistakes and make changes for the future.

Strategies for bouncing back from setbacks include reframing the situation, seeking support from others, and taking action. By reframing the situation, we can change our perspective and see setbacks as opportunities for growth and learning. Seeking support from others can provide us with guidance and encouragement, while taking action allows us to move forward and make positive changes.

The Role of Mindfulness in Building Resilience

Mindfulness is a powerful tool for managing stress and building resilience. Mindfulness involves being fully present in the moment and non-judgmentally observing our thoughts and feelings. By practicing mindfulness, we can reduce stress, improve focus, and build emotional resilience.

Techniques for practicing mindfulness include deep breathing exercises, meditation, and body scans. These techniques can help us become more aware of our thoughts and feelings, as well as reduce stress and promote relaxation. By incorporating mindfulness into our daily lives, we can build resilience and better navigate through life's challenges.

Building a Resilient Mindset for Long-Term Success

Building a resilient mindset involves developing persistence and perseverance. It is about recognizing that setbacks and failures are a normal part of life, and that they do not define us. By developing a growth mindset, we can see challenges as opportunities for growth and learning, rather than as obstacles.

Strategies for developing a growth mindset include embracing failure, seeking feedback, and focusing on the process rather than the outcome. By embracing failure, we can learn from our mistakes and make improvements for the future. Seeking feedback allows us to gain different perspectives and make necessary adjustments. Focusing on the process rather than the outcome allows us to enjoy the journey and stay motivated, even when things don't go as planned.

Thriving in the Face of Adversity

In conclusion, hope and resilience are powerful qualities that can help individuals overcome challenges and achieve success. By cultivating hope, maintaining a positive outlook, and developing coping strategies, we can build resilience and navigate through life's ups and downs. With a resilient mindset, we can bounce back from setbacks and failures, learn from our mistakes, and continue to grow and thrive. So, let us embrace hope and resilience, and continue to build a mindset that will lead us to long-term success.

Don't miss out!

Visit the website below and you can sign up to receive emails whenever Travis Breeding publishes a new book. There's no charge and no obligation.

https://books2read.com/r/B-A-CBXDB-AYHXC

BOOKS 2 READ

Connecting independent readers to independent writers.

Did you love *Beyond the Broken Mind: A Journey to Triumph Over Schizophrenia*? Then you should read *Dancing With Shadows: How To Turn Your Fears Into Powerful Allies*[1] by Travis Breeding!

[2]

Step into the captivating world of Travis Breeding as he fearlessly unveils the intricate layers of his life in 'Echoes of the Mind: A Schizophrenic's Odyssey.' In this compelling autobiography, Breeding takes readers on an extraordinary journey through the labyrinth of his mind, navigating the tumultuous terrain of schizophrenia with raw honesty and unwavering courage.

From the early whispers of auditory hallucinations to the bewildering onset of delusions, Breeding candidly shares the harrowing experiences that shaped his reality. Through the lens of his own narrative, readers gain profound insight into the inner workings of

---

1. https://books2read.com/u/bo9MkV

2. https://books2read.com/u/bo9MkV

schizophrenia, demystifying misconceptions and shedding light on the profound complexities of the human psyche.

As Breeding delves into the depths of his psyche, he unearths the poignant moments of triumph amidst adversity. Through relentless determination and unwavering resilience, he transcends the confines of his diagnosis, forging a path towards healing and self-discovery. Along the way, he grapples with the pervasive stigma surrounding mental illness, challenging societal perceptions and advocating for greater understanding and acceptance.

'Echoes of the Mind' is more than just a memoir—it is a testament to the indomitable spirit of the human experience. With poignant prose and searing authenticity, Breeding invites readers to embark on a transformative odyssey of self-reflection and empathy. This powerful memoir serves as a beacon of hope for individuals navigating the complexities of mental illness and a poignant reminder of the enduring power of the human spirit.

Read more at breedingautismconsulting.com.

Also by Travis Breeding

Harmony in Flux: Navigating Bi-Polar Brilliance
The Friendship Rainbow
The Great Kindergarten Adventure: A Story about Going to School
with Autism
The Magic Forest Adventure
Unlocking Brilliance: Navigating Autism and Applied Behavior
Analysis Towards a Radiant Future
Decoding Love: Navigating Dating and Relationships on the Autism
Spectrum
Echoes of a Late Diagnosis: Unveiling the Spectrum Within
From Theory to Practice: Implementing Effective Autism
Interventions St
The Amazing Adventures of Aiden and His Asperger's Superpowers
The Magical Adventures of Lily and the Enchanted Forest
Unlocking Potential: A Journey Of Discovery Through ABA Therapy
Unlocking Potential: Navigating Employment for Neurodiverse
Talent
Unlocking the Spectrum: A Journey through Applied Behavior
Analysis from an Autistic Perspective
Unlocking The Spectrum: Navigating The Complexity Of Autism
With Advanced Strategies And Insights
Beyond The Spectrum: Insights From Autistic Adults
Beyond The Stereotypes
Breaking Barriers: Navigating Autism With Therapeutic Insight
Celebrating Neurodiversity

About the Author

Travis is the author of over 50 books about autism spectrum disorder. He travelst he country sharing the mission of making the world a better place for autistic individuals. In his spare time Travis enjoys writing, walking, and watching sports.

Read more at breedingautismconsulting.com.